Phyllis Williams-Strawder

I AM
NOT HERE
TO FIX
MY FACE

**POSITIONING YOUR PERSONAL BRAND
TEN TOES DOWN IN YOUR BRANDED HOUSE**

I'm not here to fix my face

Positioning Your Personal Brand
Ten Toes Down In your Branded House

Phyllis Williams-Strawder

Espresso Mischief

Dedication

To the dudes in my life
for a reason, a season, or a lifetime.

My Dad, Phillip E. Williams
My Ghetto Star

My Husband, Neil P. Strawder
My Supportive Star

My Private Mentor, Eric-Quon Lee
My Guiding Star

My Public Mentor, Chris Do
My Challenging Star

My Perfectionist, Vanja Stojanović
My Designing Star

Contents

Don't allow your personal brand to consume your personal life. Giving access to your life and loved one is granting permission you may not want others to have or that you can't handle.

Last but not least, I wanna thank me
I wanna thank me for believing in me
I wanna thank me for doing all this hard work
I wanna thank me for having no days off
I wanna thank me for, for never quitting

I wanna thank me for always being a giver
And tryna give more than I receive
I wanna thank me for tryna do more right than
wrong
I wanna thank me for just being me at all times
Snoop Dogg, you a bad Motha Fucka

- Snoop Dogg, I Wanna Thank Me

RBF of A Personal Brand

Marketing a business brands service or product has always been about the P's; product, packaging, placement, promotion, etc. Then 25 years ago, Tom Peters wrote, The Brand You 50. A book about transforming from an "Employee" to a brand. Ever since then, folx have been peddling their asses for every thing from a job to a date and calling it personal branding.

Personal branding was never one of the P's of marketing. A big reason for that is because folx got caught up in marketing themselves like employees. The common phrase of, "I am the brand" spread like a bad rash. For someone who's self-employed, like an influencer, that's fine. For someone who is entrepreneur-ial, like the Founder of a scalable service-based business, it's a train wreck waiting to happen.

The carnage of being the brand has left a trail of burnt out, overwhelmed, and over worked folx. People became products and tried to fill all the other P roles. Promote yourself, package yourself, place yourself on all the platforms. And let's not forget pricing yourself by charging your worth. All this is an effort to be a brand.

Everyone with a following has advice on being a brand. Well, no more. All of it is an attempt to figuratively fix your resting bitch face.

***

Yes, personal branding is a BITCH and it comes with a resting bitch face.

My first year at UCLA is when I noticed a bitch following me. Folx mistook my reclusiveness and neutral demeanor as me being an uppity bitch. The truth was I was an insecure 18 year old girl who felt awkward and out of place.

When I was in my twenties I was notorious for pairing my long legs with short skirts. Knowing I would attract unwanted attention didn't stop me from it though. Saying no to the unwanted attention most times came with the retaliatory word of bitch.

Despite feeling awkwardly tall compared to the short boys and men trying to get at me, my desire to be left alone was met with bad tempers and that bitch. It got so bad I started saying yes just to avoid the confrontation.

After a while being called a bitch got old and played out. I don't remember where I heard it but my response became, "I've been called worse things by better people."

It lessened the sting and I began to give less fucks.

***

Did you know resting bitch face is a real thing studied by behavioral scientists, Abbe McBeth and Jason Rogers? I won't go down the rabbit hole but I want you to think of every time someone stranger told you to smile. That's them telling you to fix your resting bitch face. When clients come with money in hand they have a similar expectation.

Despite your lofty title of Founder, CEO, or Grand Pubah, potential clients expect you to fix your face. If you don't, they will take their money elsewhere. And business being what it is, most will comply. But what about those rebellious creatures who say fuck you and your money?

How can you build an empire that let's you keep your resting bitch face? Own the reality of what a bitch does without permission that pisses everyone off. As Founder, establish boundaries, be clear in your broadcast, and build bridges to folx you wanna be bothered with. Three big B's.

The usual suspects of personal branding are to market yourself, hype yourself, and humanize yourself by sharing your personal life. That's not branding, that's attention seeking. I know you can do better than that. You're a fucking entrepreneur.

For a long time the gold standard of personal branding was set by rich, white, businessmen. The usual suspects being Jeff Bezos, Richard Branson, Steve Jobs and the like. I won't argue my point of people vs. brands because that's not the point of this book. The point is that personal brands are a valuable asset in an attention seeking world.

Positioning your personal brand as an authority and expert is not about getting attention. You don't have to fix your face or play nice. It's about taking up space as a brand leader, not a business owner. And it definitely isn't about hiding behind a mission statement of bullshit. That's just something you were told to make up using one of the many templates that go like this:

1. What do you do?
2. Why do you do it?
3. Who do you do it for?

Mission statements are just a corporate mind fuck to get buyers to trust a business that is more concerned with profit margins than people. If I'm lying then you wouldn't see owners building space ships while their employees try to make rent. Amazon's current mission statement is, "to be Earth's most customer-centric company," I'm not a space nut, but is Jeff gearing up for Prime delivery to other planets?

Nevertheless, it's time for founders of independent businesses to stop using corporate roadmaps of crazy. I mean, unless your goal is to be one a transactional company driven only by data. Corporate methodology comes with a built-in mindset that you have to compete for every client or sale. You're brainwashed that there is financial scarcity in a world of over 8 billion people. While you're competing with folx who don't know you exist, big business continues to horde the wealth and dictate terms.

Let me tell you something. Competition in business is for the greedy. It means you're trying to take something away from someone else. Or you're trying to keep someone else from getting ahead. My only question is why? Sweetheart, on your worse day in business, the most you have to contend with, is being an alternative when someone is looking for a solution. The market is not saturated but it's full of folx who are play'n at business. They will forever have a side hustle because they're afraid to go all in. That's not you.

So what is your personal brand solution in a supposed competitive market? You fix your face, become a one person content machine and turn your life into content. You shine a light on your awards and mentions to be seen as an "authority" in the industry. You comment on everything that's even remotely relevant to be seen as an "expert." You do all that and still ask your audience, "What do you want me to do next?"

You ask what's next because you don't see the true brilliance of your resting bitch face. You know what everyone else does in your position does? Ask the same damn question and get the same damn answer. Where's the youniqueness in all of it? It can be found in the RBF of your personal brand.

Personal brand youniqueness is not found in authenticity. Authenticity is an innate version of your truth. It's a you only thing. Folx have worn the "A" off of the word by trying to convince others that they're not fake. If you have to tell folx you're authentic then evidently it's hiding behind a fixed face. On top of that, authenticity doesn't position a personal brand in any shape, form, or fashion.

Personal brand positioning doesn't require a spotlight. Your position as an authority, expert, and leader is illuminated by the boundaries, broadcast, and bridges of the personal brand. The original marketing P's are not the same for a personal brand. The first clue is that you're not a **product** or service. And despite folx telling you to market yourself and charge your worth, you were not born with a **price** in mind.

That's two P's gone right there. What about **promoting** yourself. That's arrogant and or cringy if done wrong. And then there's **placement**, showing up on all the social media platforms like a product on a shelf. Those P's scream burnout.

So then what IS the deal with positioning a personal brand? It's about standing ten toes down, resting bitch face and all, with a personal brand as THE parent brand..It's attracts clients and talent alike for company and revenue growth. It's showing up as an endorser brand as well as being influential instead of hiring an influencer.

Founders of a serviced-based business can creatively range from the kitchen to the classroom. And yet, big business bullies, who want to sell you on their platforms, have you chasing authenticity and algorithms with constant content creation. Aren't you already doing the most without having to shove a camera in your face for the sake of content? Maybe it's just me. I know it's not and it's why the **personal brand positioning** of the PB&Slay framework gets my clients excited. They begin to see how the C.O.D.E. and C.A.M.P. pieces strategically fit.

As the former success of being Mrs. Mista of Bigmista's to the success of the Ghetto Country Brandmother® of Brandma's House, the lessons learned to personal branding and staying true to self came hard. Finding an alternative approach to always being on and intruding on my life was a necessity. I didn't want to experience another identity crisis like I did with Mrs. Mista.

Implementing a positioning framework that included deeper boundaries, broadcasting, and bridge building gave me the courage to be vocal, visible, and vigilant. That's what I'm sharing in this book so you can stand ten toes down in your own branded house, not just rent social media space.

Sharing the overall C.O.D.E., C.A.M.P., and P.L.A.Y. process with clients showed me that it doesn't have to be done in order. You can mix it up so you stay C.A.L.M. You can set up for a C.O.M.E. back. You can even remix for a C.L.A.P. back. But whatever you do, you have to be positioned so you don't have to fix your face for folx.

Here it is: A strong personal brand attracts a target audience. Within that audience is an ideal client. Not THE ideal client because those are as rare as unicorn shit dusted with rainbow glitter. Your personal brand can convey a message that imagery and words on a website cannot. You trust the business is established through the genuine sincerity of what your personal brand represents.

You become a leader in your field, industry, or market. And what's often overlooked is that a strategic personal brand paves the way for market expansion that opens doors to new opportunities beyond your current reach. Sounds pretty damn good, right?

Let's take it to the domino table for a minute. If you get five say, nick 'em don't cut 'em. If you get ten, say TENtion. But if you get fifteen, slam your bone down and say, three switch'n bitches. Bitch was how we started this game so it seems fitting to end it that way. They won't see it coming when you nick 'em with **boundaries**, you'll get some TENtion when you **broadcast**, and to win the game you build a **bridge**. Even if you never play dominoes you'll forever remember three switch'n bitches and how it relates to personal brand positioning.

- **Boundaries:** Throw away the tired notion of competition and focus on building **boundaries of separation**, not barriers. You're not in a race, and there's no point chasing an invisible competitor. Identify what makes you younique and plant your flag. Leverage strengths that show you as a game changer instead of a game player.

- **Broadcasting:** Delivering your message consistently and effectively is key. It's about **being able to broadcast** regularly. You craft a never-ending story of a growing business that attracts an ideal audience. The value of the overall brand architecture is baked into that broadcast.

- **Bridges:** Getting an audience to see the value of your overall brand architecture requires **a bridge to close the gap**. It's not that everyone in the audience who crosses will buy but at the very least, they will remember. It's that sweet spot of sharing, education, and intrigue that makes them want to crossover.

I would never hint about you making someone your bitch or that you are a bitch. This is about the perception that branding and marketing hang their hat on. It's an, I don't give a fuck what they say when I'm not in the room vibe. If you're afraid of that, then this book is not for you.

On the other hand, if you want to be connected to your business through a personal brand and not chained to it with your personal life, keep reading. Making that happen is what this book is about. It's written for folx who want return to the joy and excitement of why they chose entrepreneurship.

If after reading this book you find yourself struggling to position your personal brand go back and read my book, Branding, Boundaries, & Bullshit. This book is a breakdown of the "P" in setting up C.A.M.P. of PB&Slay. The core message you broadcast from is based on the DNA C.O.D.E. of the personal brand. This not about chasing trends, doing market research, or hiding behind filters. It's not about B2B or B2C. It's about person to person.

So let's do this.

"In the black culture, certain kids are given nicknames that they roll with forever; the nicknames outweigh their real names. I'm one of those scenarios."

- Snoop Dogg, Esquire

I Respectfully Rebel

I was raised on ass whoop'ns, respect your elders, and fix your face.

"You better fix your face." Boy does that bring back memories of chest heaving sobs with your arms folded in defiance. If your mama said that, it was because you were STILL crying after being chastised or you were mean muggin' like you could whoop her. Either way you knew your mama wasn't play'n.

Fixing your face was never about putting a smile on your lips. It was a warning to fix your attitude. I didn't fully understand it until I became a parent and disciplined my own daughter. Yes, I still believe in ass whoop'ns but only as a last resort. Those that have a problem with it so what.

What I remember most about becoming the disciplinarian is

falling victim to fear. Fear of her getting hurt in any shape, form, or fashion. Fear that if I didn't discipline her now, a cruel world would try to do it later. Discipline seemed a safer lesson than cruelty. Thats how I learned that fear is often masked as anger.

Me angrily yelling at my daughter because I was afraid for her safety. My daughter angrily glaring at me because she was afraid of messing up again and knowing she unintentionally would.

I can't remember when I flipped from telling her to "fix yo face" to "You ain't gotta fix your face for nobody, not even me. Just don't be disrespectful." I can't remember the last disciplinary ass whoop'n, but I remember why. It was a matter of letting her mature and own who she wants to be in this world. Yes, I will respect it but this is still my house.

As a Founder not only do you want the freedom of entrepreneurship, you want the respect as well. You open a door to your personal life looking for acceptance instead of respecting the privacy of your personal life. It's because you're brainwashed to believe in order for your audience to know, like, and trust they need to see how you live.. You may as well bend over and say, I can take it, as you fix your face in preparation to get fucked. You're giving them what they want instead with little regard for what you want.

Them are the social media platforms and content carnivores that follow you to ease their boredom. You follow trends, adapt to algorithms, and consistently cultivate irrelevant content. You're doing everything accept what you want to do which is blaze trails, lift as you climb, brand by example. You continuously have to fix your face to keep up because if you don't the algorithm will ignore you and your audience won't engage. Scroll through and what you see is bunch of hot mess content or boring business owners. Prime example of fix your face is Snoop on LinkedIn with 200k followers vs. his profile on Instagram with over 87M followers.

I mean, let's keep it 100. Those who aren't willing to fix their face for the cause have a running theme of being too cultural, rebellious, or profane. How dare you bring your shenanigans in this house (on this platform). It's giving LeBron should just shut up and dribble vibe or Colin should stand the fuck up energy. Personally, I've tried to pay to boost my content and they won't even take my money.

So yes, they let Snoop bring his brand name to the LinkedIn, however, they told him to check his shenanigans at the door. His content is very well-behaved. Reading it you don't even hear Snoop's voice. Y'all know Snoop will drop nigga bombs in a heartbeat. I dare you to find it in his content on LinkedIn. His social media manager is following all the rules of community respectability.

I know some of you will jump on your professional high horse and say he shouldn't use words like that on such a platform. My questions is why not? I know there's a time and place for everything but in the world of social media marketing and personal branding you're punished for not conforming. Even more egregious are the same professional mofo's screaming how authentic they are will tell others to lessen their authenticity. Miss me with the sanctimonious bullshit.

This is why some of you don't know how to show up. You don't wanna "fix your face" but you don't wanna be left out. So what do you do? You either do nothing or you push out well behaved content by code-switching or tempering your message. All the while you're asking folx how to get more leads.

So while I respect ALL mothers, I'm not here to fix my face and I'm not asking you to fix yours. I'm here to stand ten toes down in my truth, to show how to position your personal brand in a way that is unshakeable, unfiltered, and unapologetic. In other words, be respectfully rebellious because the moment you start fixing your face for the masses, becomes the moment you start losing pieces of yourself. You dilute your message, your energy and your level of impact.

Authenticity is the buzzword that got you here, but it is not the word keeping you here. You showed up with your quirks, coolness, and keepsakes because it's where you're most comfort- able. You're willing to say what needs to be said for the audience you want to attract. You don't want to be just another watered down version of respectable corporate crazy.

You've been inspired over the years by change makers and proverbial rump shakers in the game. They're noisy, well rounded and fluid. They're a remix of rebel and visionary because they dare to be distinct. They don't fix their face for the crowd, they stick out their chin and say fuck around and find out.

This book is for you who respectfully rebel against trend chasing, data digs, and gap filling. It's for folx who want to position their personal brands as courageous communicators. It's not about pushing boundaries or cultural disruption. It's taking a firm stand behind boundaries of your own making. It's about finding strength in what brings you joy. It's about building a bridge between the audience and the offer.

Ditch the well-behaved content, embrace your truth, and position your personal brand ten toes down because in a world that is constantly telling you to fix your face, it time for YOU to stick out your chin so they can fuck around and find out.

***

Location, location, location. That's how a real estate agent sells you. Do you wanna be near good schools, night life, shopping? What? When you want to sell someone on an offer, where is your personal brand located in relation? Is it non-existent, barely there, or trying to be authentic? Prime real estate in the mind of your audience is better held by people in the industry, not their offers.

Positioning is one of the marketing P's that wasn't referenced earlier even though this book is about positioning. And just like real estate, the value of brand positioning is found in the location to desired proximity. But the value of a personal brand requires different parameters of a business brand. At the same time it works as an endorser brand by facilitating the P's of marketing for the business.

Taking up space as the brand confuses all of this. You're marketing yourself as the solution instead of endorsing the solution. As the founder of a company, you don't use the P's of marketing on yourself. As the Founder you promote, package, price, and position the various products and offers of the business brand(s).

Personal Brands don't have the same qualities as a product or service. So why are you being told to position YOURSELF as a commodity? You're the founder of a business with expectations of growing, scaling, and expanding. Where you position in the mind of your audience requires a more strategic, yet visceral approach. It will reduce the urge to ignore you because it leverages human bias.

If you're not stepping up to the mic to endorse your business, then you're hard pressed to make the P's work in your favor. The P's were conceived for corporate giants to get in your head. They used research and data, that is not totally unbiased, to manufacture a persona that supposedly represents 'you' as an ideal client. Based on that, they create ads so you convince yourself they're talking to you. It's all smoke and mirrors to increase the bottom line.

You can test this by check'n out Walmart. They attracted media attention because they are switching up their brand to attract more 'affluent' customers. Their marketing strategy will use a mix of the P's minus the one you have in your favor. The Personal Brand.

Using traditional marketing methods, let's break apart Walmart's positioning beginning with a change in value proposition and differentiation.

- **Value Prop:** This is supposed to be the golden ticket. It's supposed to answer the question "why them?" What do they do that is so great you forget about every other store in the marketplace? A lot of their value was wrapped up in "Rollback" prices. That's not a go to selling point for the affluent especially for a store not commonly found in their neighborhood. In my mind I see it as gentrification of the general store. They're ditching the folx that kept them occupied to target those who can pay more. So then, what's the new value?
- **Differentiation:** Once in a class all by itself, they are now aiming to be like Target - said with a bad French accent. They're trading their current number one position to become second to an existing brand. What happens to the positioning of their celebrity brand partners like Drew Barrymore, Sofia Vergara, or Paris Hilton? They can't hold a candle to the Disney, Starbucks, Apple experience of Target. So then, what the new differentiator?

Next on the Walmart agenda is changing their actual positioning framework of audience, competition, and persona.
- **Audience:** They can't be everything to everyone, so in comes

the one ring to rule them all. They do research, crunch data, and create detailed buyer personas to represent demographics, needs, wants, and pain points. That's how they'll come up with their affluent customer model.

- **Competition:** Who are they up against? Top of mind for me is Target. But what is their SWOT compared to them? They compare all this information to find holes to fill and opportunities to pounce on a money maker. Target has nothing to worry about because of Walmart's tarnished history.
- **Voice and Personality:** Think of a Walmart commercial compared to one for Target. The first gives Everyman archetype vibe where the later is Everyman with an undertone of Creator. Their communication tone and style across touchpoints, from marketing materials to social media engagement is tame compared to Target.

Five of the P's play a role in this marketing strategy. It's about filling supposed gaps in the market place. Each one trying to get in where they fit in. The trickiest one is pricing unless it's a luxury brand. But never underestimate a good sale. Nevertheless, there's a method to the madness of brand positioning for a company.

- **Clarity and Focus:** A well-defined brand position makes marketing a lot easier. Knowing the market and the value the business provides hits home with folx.
- **Connection:** Strong brand positioning builds an emotional

connections to folx. They feel seen, heard, and understood. Aligning with the brand persona and the proposed solution, they're more likely to become loyal brand advocates.

- **Decision-Making:** Effective brand positioning puts folx in the right frame of mind so your marketing strategy makes your pricing strategy look good. When folx can't make up their mind, they rely on the brand to do it for them.

I want you to marinate on this before we move on. There are two luxury car brands. Brand A positions as the leader in cutting-edge technology and innovation, targeting tech-savvy folx who value performance and the latest gadgets. Brand B, on the other hand, focuses on timeless design, heritage, and crafts-manship, appealing to folx who prioritize luxury and tradition. If you're a car enthusiast, it will be easy for you to identify two cars that fit the bill.

According to Statista.com, "The luxury car segment made up about 4.5 percent of the light vehicle market in the United States in June 2021…" With such a small footprint a lot of you may have come up with the same cars just not in the same order.

Because the world won't stop spinning, brand positioning is a continuous process. As industries evolve and new alternatives emerge, refining your personal brand position to stay relevant is a must. And because big business is always in competition, someone has to come out on top.

In Branding, Boundaries, & Bullshit, I talk about Personal

Brand Ego. It's about boundaries and how you set up C.A.M.P. The "P" being positioning. Surrounding your personal brand with the right kinda of content, audience, marketing, and positioning insulates you from fuckery and fakeness.

Positioning is the final boundary because it's where you dig in to reinforce that you're putting down roots as an **authority, expert, and leader** in the industry or marketplace. And you're doing it on your terms. You never have to move but you continuously adapt to changing conditions.

All this lets you know that you're not a brand and you're not in competition. When you have to worry about stakeholders, stockholders, and board members, then you can worry about this type of marketing and brand positioning. Until then, this is not your problem.

"You might not have a car or a big gold chain, stay true to yourself and things will change."

- Snoop Dogg

BOUNDARIES

Boundaries were not my thing growing up. I was all about the barriers back then. It came from a fear of confrontation. Witnessing physical in our home growing up had a lot to do with it. I was grown with my first marriage in my rearview mirror when barriers shifted to boundaries.

For years I had relied on barriers which blocked a lot of good from getting in OR out. Those same barriers kept all the bad inside. It made me feel less than about myself. I had a lotta hard head makes a soft behind lessons before I really got it.

When I left the restaurant industry for coaching those old barriers tried to come back. And that's how boundaries in personal branding became a thing.

Be A Niche Of One

Whether you bootstrapped, got a loan, or had investors, you started this business to build something. You've poured your heart, soul, and kitchen sink into do'n the damn thing. You know you're talented, you offer incredible value, but frustration sets in because shit's not pop'n like you want.

In the sphere of personal branding the constant message of be authentic and hype yourself has become white noise. If it were true you wouldn't have to chase trends and you wouldn't get lost in a sea of sameness. So instead of making money, you're competing for followers based on dancing, pointing, and spilling your guts.

The truth about personal branding that's being ignored is that, there is no reason to compete for follows, likes, or anything else. You use it as the ultimate inbound marketing asset to generate leads that generate revenue. It's time to stop with the know, like, and trust bullshit. Your personal brand is your moneymaker. It's not about jumping on a trends, it's about blazing trails. You can do that with an audience of one or ten thousand and one. It's all in the youniqueness.

Developing a boundary of youniqueness is how you begin to take root. Call it a Younique Strategy. It's how you show up to your happy place. And being in that happy place gives you the courage, if not the confidence, to just be in the moment of doing what you do. You ditch the competitive mindset because you got shit to do.

Picture your happy place as a wide open space for you to play in. The only problem is that it's open to everyone so you feel judged and watched. So instead of enjoying your happy place you're watching to see who's watching you. Who's trying to steal your joy?

Your first thought is to put up barriers. With barriers nothing can get in, but that also means nothing can get out. When you add an entryway, you turn barriers into boundaries.

In the real world of open spaces, boundaries can include things like hedges, set points, or landmarks. In personal branding boundaries are built with **hyphens**, **strengths**, and **language**. These boundaries make it easy for folx to get in and you to get out. They keep your happy place happy, your content consistent, and your audience in attendance. I had none of this when I began my journey in personal branding.

When I started the barbecue business with my husband back in 2006, I was cool because we were low-key. But when we made it official, like sign on the dotted line, I became a straight hater. I saw everyone in the barbecue business as an enemy. I had no problem with my husband flirting with women but he better NOT talk to another barbecue person. Yeah, I was that kinda crazy.

It kinda, only kinda, makes sense since our business was literally birthed from doing barbecue competitions. Before we started selling barbecue I loved most of the folx. It's a community filled with camaraderie, cheering, and support. But then there's the secret side. Sauces, rubs, and techniques were carefully guarded and we were no different.

After a while, I developed a disdain for barbecue competitions. The judging seemed totally unfair to me. But that's another story for another day. What kept us on the circuit was the People's Choice category. We weren't always a hit with the judges but we won more than our fair share of People's Choice Awards. After a while I only focused on winning People's Choice. They could keep the rest.

Unlike most of the competitors, Neil and I engaged with the folx in line. We danced, we joked, we hugged. It wasn't a ploy to garner favor, we just truly appreciated folx willing to stand in line for our food. And I honestly can't tell you if folx voted for us more for the food or because they liked us. Either way, no one could compete with Bigmista and Mrs. Mista on that level.

Here's the crazy part. When we focused on doing our thing at the competition, the competition fell off. Not because they couldn't compete but because in the grand scheme of things it didn't matter. In those moments of jokes, hugs, and dancing, we weren't out to beat anyone, we were just having fun and sharing the love. When I looked back, I saw the lesson: when it comes to personal branding, competition is a dead end.

Worrying about the other teams as rivals did absolutely nothing to up our game. Engaging with the audience as Bigmista and Mrs. Mista were moments of joy that could have been wasted on worry about "the competition". It makes an already stressful experience worse because you forget this is supposed to be my happy place.

Seeing everyone in your industry as competition is a trap. You and others in the industry are fighting over supposed scraps while big businesses get bigger. It's scarcity mindset 101. It blinds you to the fact that your personal brand can make a deeper connection than a big brand that's been around for years. And no one can take whats meant for you.

Looking at your personal brand through the lens of corporate tactics and authentic behavior will stress you the fuck out. Even if you're competitive by nature, what are you winning? It's a flawed lens that keeps you stuck in a game with no end because there's always someone better.

Here's the liberating truth. You can't control what others do or think. You can't run your business around your frenemies strategies, prices, or offers. You can only control your brand architecture. Look at Beyonce and Taylor Swift no competition. It's the Beehive and Swifties who have beef with each other. That's how deep brand loyalty runs.

Think about it another way. Are you drawn to generic restaurants with seemingly identical menus? Or are you more likely to be captivated by a place with a distinct ambiance, a signature dish that pushes boundaries, and a passionate chef whose love for food spills over onto every plate? The generic restaurants try to thrive on imitation and fuckery. And yet, if they attempt to focus on being "better" than the others, they lose sight of their true value.

Success, whatever that looks like for you, lies in embracing your younique strengths, secret spice, or unconventional sprinkles. It's about building a personal brand that attracts and connect with your ideal audience, the folx who appreciate your get down even if it's not theres. That's where the magic happens, not in the aisles of discount competitors.

Sweetheart, in this day and age your biggest competition is the internet. Can you say Google, Youtube, or AI? And no matter how many folx search or prompt to find out how you do what you do, they can't do it like you. And they definitely can't lead it like you. That's because they try to apply the tactics based on theory. Making it happen in real life is the true test of youniqueness.

If you read some of the same authors I did, Marty Neumeier, Seth Godin, and the guys whose who starts with Why, everything they talk about flies under the banner of all the corporations they've worked with. They wouldn't even touch a company of your size unless you were a friend. All they know is how to compete. It's the life blood of a toxic work culture. It's limited bitch ass thinking. The world of big business as fraught with hierarchy, evaluations, and inequality. All in an effort to make you work for "it." Whatever *it* is.

Profits are tied to a stock price. If you're a business owner with stock price issues then you're out of my league. I'm just say'n. And even if that's where you're headed, you're not there yet. You're starting this game from the YOU level. So you as the Founder have to stand as a brand leader, not a business owner.

On your worst day in business, the only thing someone else can offer a potential client is an **alternative** to what you offer. You might be feeling insecure, comparing your services to the next "guru" online, but the reality is you're not in competition. You're simply offering an alternative to what else is out there. And don't call it a better alternative because then you have to ask, who's better than you. And you're right back in competition mode.

If you ditch the competitive mindset you can focus on engaging with your with your audience. Outside of bargain shoppers, most folx who are afraid to admit they have a problem are looking for folx who speak their language. The youniqueness of your personal brand can crack that first barrier of skepticism.

But because folx are drowning in a SEO sea of sameness, they settle for something else based on price. May as well get the biggest bang for their buck. But what they really wanted was some real talk and results.

Target audiences are overflowing with ideal clients who aren't comparison shopping. They're looking for alternatives to the okie doke. They're not interested in the business that bought its way to the top of Google. They want the brand that's an SEO all its own. If you build it, you have to lead it, and they will follow.

Some leaders are born, some are made. It doesn't matter how you became a leader as long as you stand ten toes down as one. If leading makes you uncomfortable, I promise, it will show in your bottom line. And if I've learned anything after all these years, leading is not the same as bossing. Look it up.

In personal branding, you want to find your leadership style to establish boundaries. There are assessments, quizzes, test and a whole host of ways to find your leadership style. In personal branding, it's a dual role of business and brand. That's hard to do when marketing "experts" keep relegating you people pleasing. The irony that they utter this in the same breath as authenticity and differentiation is fuckery personified.

Y'all already know from my book, Balance Is Bullshit, I'm that literal bitch. So the duplicitous bullshit of authenticity and people-pleasing cannot co-exist unless you're a natural people-pleaser. It flies in the face of staying true to you and genuine with your audience. Maybe it's the rebel in me, but why start a business only to ask permission on how to proceed?

Folx constantly talk about disruption in the branding space and yet they hide from it. The most disruptive personal brands I know come from the rap industry. But since most didn't know how to capitalize on their name outside the music industry, they fizzled out. Others became music producers, but then there are the rebellious few that won't go out like punks.

Tracy Lauren Morrow, O'Shea Jackson Sr., Dana Elaine Owens, Clifford Smith, Jr., Calvin Cordozar Broadus, Jr. IYKYK. So let's talk about it.

The Rap game is a personal brand gold mine but no one ever sees rappers as examples of brands or business outside of the music genre. The industry itself is ripe with rebellious archetypes and maybe that's why no one goes there. If rappers took up space with personal branding, what would the landscape look like now? I can't call it but I can talk about it.

Early in my personal branding career even I ignored the lyrical elephants in the room. When asked about top personal brands, I was often at a loss. I was trying so hard to get away from names like Steve Jobs and Richard Branson, I couldn't open my mind to see outside of big business. Even as a hard core Rap fan the constant drumming of rich white dudes was firmly positioned in my branded brain.

The rap genre has been doing the damn thing since Sugar Hill Gang. Wonder Mike, Master Gee, and Big Hank were personal brand pioneers. Then there's Public Enemy. Flava Flav squandered his name on a dumb ass show. Terminator X and Chuck D could have done some brand damage, in a good way, if they had known to capitalize on their names.

Then there's NWA, Nigga's With Attitude. Eazy E, DJ Yella, MC Ren, Ice Cube and Dr. Dre started but who was left standing? Dr. Dre dominated the music industry as an artist and producer. He's a straight up shot caller, yet no one ever mentions his personal brand. Beats by Dre anyone? Ice Cube went from rap anarchist to entrepreneurial activist. Despite his personal brand name not being on any of his businesses, the name recognition opened doors for him to take up space. Did you know dude launched an E&J Brandy brand called Fifth Generation?

What opened my eyes to all of this was Snoop Dogg doing an ad where he said he was giving up smoke. Folx lost their shit. Everybody knows Snoop is known for his weed consumption. It was a great marketing ploy that fell flat. I could go into reasons why but that's outside the scope of this book. The thing is when Snoop Dogg came on the scene he brought his weed with him.

The message behind each person I mentioned can be found in their lyrics. How folx connected with them and their rap message can be seen and felt because it hasn't change. The stand outs in the few I've mentioned are Ice Cube and Snoop. In Ice Cube's case, he's still fighting the same fight when he said, "Fuck the police" it's just on a broader scale of equity. Snoop on the other hand is still smoke'n his weed and is besties with a rich, white, fellow felon.

The youniqueness of Ice Cube and Snoop allow them to take up space. If Ice Cube is positioned as a parent brand, then Big 3 and Fifth Generation would be part of a house of brands.

Snoop, on the other hand is a whole ass empire. Positioned as a parent brand, Snoop Dogg has a hybrid house of sub-brands that include Leafs by Snoop, Snoopadelic Films, and the Snoopify App. Digital Dogg is his animation company. Indoggo Gin, spelled with the D O double G. He partnered with his wife to develop Broadus Foods. Snoop Doggie Doggs is a pet product brand. Martha Stewart is his go to for collaborations. I love their partnership with Bic to launch Best Buds Bag. And his recent licensing deal with Skechers is all the things.

Snoop is a whole ass case study of personal branding. If not for his name and weed tendencies, he would be dismissed as just another dope smoke'n brotha. Unlike the aforementioned Steve Jobs, Jeff Bezos, and Richard Branson, Snoop had to separate the who from the do but still remain true. He monetized the name Snoop Dogg with a blunt in his hand. That's ten toes down kinda shit.

Jeff Bezos was 30 when he started Amazon in 1994. Snoop Dogg was 21 when he started rapping in 1992. Makes you think, doesn't it. I'm not going to bring up inequality because that's my personal fight, not my business one. But heres something to ponder. If the seed for branding and endorsements were planted and nurtured in Snoop like they were in athletes of his time, where would he be now?

Your personal brand, with boundaries, is your chance to play the game on your terms. When you stop competing for something that can't be taken from you, generating revenue becomes easier. Folx stop finding reasons not to pay you and get creative about how they'll pay you. This is not manifesting abundance bullshit. This is intentional and strategic which is how you do business.

If you think of the world in terms of having alternatives, you will see the abundance. You can't make someone choose you but you can offer them the choice. I've seen folx stay loyal to something that wasn't serving them because it fits "the devil you know" scenario. In other words they're lazy or complacent. You can't compete with that.

The world at large conditions you to compete. As a black person I was told I had to be twice as good to get half as much. Then the seed was planted for being crabs in a barrel. So now everyone who wants what I want is holding me back. It's brainwashing 101. You see it in individuals from the boardroom to the bedroom. From procreating to parenting.

Despite the so-called "authenticity" factor of personal branding, folx still feel the need to compete. You put up barriers instead of boundaries. Is it any wonder the same thing is ringing in your ear about personal branding? If you put up boundaries, you play the game on your terms. You **refine the alternative**. The constant maturing of a brand leader.

Snoop is a refined alternative of what is available in the marketplace. His personal brand has expanded beyond the Rap game and the Snoop Dogg parent brand is positioned as a brand leader. It's a refined rebellious alternative that goes beyond the basic notion of differentiation. It's created depth and dimension into a personal brand that no longer relies on rapping skills. He is the D O double G for life, but he will leave a legacy with everything that came after.

Continuous maturing adaptability of a personal brand as a refined alternative keeps you from being irrelevant and forgettable. If you settle for different then you're thinking short-term. It's momentary attention in a sea of sameness until the outside noise starts bleeding in. You end up right back at the starting line with everyone else. It's the boundaries of hyphens, strengths, and languages that keep your audience fresh and fluid.

Consider this last thing. Every rapper has their own style. Snoop and Dr. Dre both have a low-key almost zen like cadence to their lyrical game. But where Snoop gives off an, I don't give a fuck vibe, Dr. Dre offers you a serving of authority and confidence. That's because both men stand on their own merits in the same game. They don't compete or copy each other, but both are youniquely recognizable.

This same principle applies in personal branding when you look through the lens of boundaries and refined alternatives. Say you're a private chef. What sets you apart? Are you known for your banana puddin? Do you dance while you dish; make up songs about food; tell endless stories about family and food? Identifying your younique flavor is how you refine the alternative and position the personal brand for authority, expertise, and leadership.

Understanding that your personal brand is in constant refinement mode makes room to adapt while you stand firm. Trends, filters, and gurus be damned. The genuineness of the personal brand approach increases trust without trying so fucking hard.

Personal branding is rooted in personal development. And as long as you're open to constant refinement, your role as the parent brand will make room for opportunities, for you and the business.

"I tell the truth. And I know what I'm talking about. That's why I'm a threat."

- *Snoop Dogg*

Hyphens As Your Hedge

What do you think of when you think of hedges. I have a dirty mind so if someone talked about getting their "hedge trimmed," you know where my mind would go. But I seriously digress.

Hyphens, like hedges, need to be maintained. They are the first step in reinforcing boundaries. Whether you're multi passionate or have varying intersections, you use hyphens to try and capture everything about you. How many hyphens do you currently have in your social media bio? You want to be recognized for all your roles, labels, and accolades. They're an attempt to compress your life for folx who don't give a shit.

You compress your perceived identity into hyphens as a means to define yourself and your worth. Over hyphenating can sends a message of insecurity. I've seen hyphens on LinkedIn that start with familial titles before career titles. What I see is a person who's afraid they're going to prioritize business over babies. Another may start with being number one or award-winning to send a message or importance. What I see is a person whose self- esteem is wrapped up in their accomplishments and accolades.

Those hyphens are a compressed identity that you use to define YOURSELF. In addition to what you do, you want to identify the most important roles in your life. You're trying to capitalize on that fucked up know, like, trust shit because you think it will make you seem more "authentic." Folx aren't looking to define you. They want to **describe** you when they're making references or referrals.

So much of who you are is wrapped in a blanket of labels. Some labels were given to you by others. Some you gave to yourself. Years, maybe even generations, of conditioning has told you that those labels are how the world knows who you are. What if I told you that's not who you are but it's how you identify? Those identities either group you or separate you from others around you.

There are visible and invisible identifiers. The visible ones are the first things folx notice about you. Listing the invisible ones seems like a low-key attempt at separating you from your haters.

NEWSFLASH: It won't work

I met a white woman some years ago and we were having a great conversation until she said, "Oh, my husband is black." My response was, "So is mine. So what?" She felt she had to qualify an already genuine conversation with the label of 'married to a black man'. It brought no value to the space and created an awkward situation for her.

Wanting folx to know the invisible parts of you so you can feel seen is you seeking validation, not income. Wanting folx to know the invisible things about you so you feel valued is you being complacent, not connected. It does nothing for your personal brand except make people wonder what any of it has to do with your business.

Using hyphens that don't provide a visible and interesting value add, limit your expansion. Some of you are looking for brand deals with generic identifiers. They're not part of your hype game at all. What made me go full tilt on Snoop Dogg's personal brand was the "giving up smoke" ad that fell flat

The company Snoop partnered with was trying to capitalize on something that didn't fit their brand. It ended up blowing up in their face. The misalignment and press coverage was not kind. It damaged their brand, but didn't do shit to Snoop.

Snoops personal brand identity is woven with **weed and words**. Those are just two of his visible hyphens. When weed became legal in California Snoop was probably ahead of the game. I'm not a weed smoker, so I don't know. And did he know when he did Gin and Juice that he would create his gin brand Indoggo?

Snoops licensing deal with Bic is brand magic because they wanted to partner with him, not be endorsed by him. That means they use his likeness and he never has to say a word. On top of that he did a collab with BFF Martha Stewart to do another deal with Bic for the "Best Buds Bag" where the latch holds the Bic lighter. The pockets inside hold your weed.

That's some brand expansion for your ass but it's not all. There are several versions of the bag inspired by Snoop and Martha's refreshed BIC EZ Reach Lighter designs. They were slated to drop this earlier this year but I can't find them anywhere. If you see one get it for me and I'll CashApp you.

Queen Latifah (Dana Owens) is another one who holds it down with a personal brand. Her business game ain't as strong as Snoop's, but ol gurl did get her own talk show. That's not what does for me though. It's that she keeps her personal life private

In a 2008 New York Times interview she told 'em, "I don't have a problem discussing the topic of somebody being gay, but I do have a problem discussing my personal life. You don't get that part of me. Sorry. We're not discussing it in our meetings, I don't feel like I need to share my personal life, and I don't care if people think I'm gay or not. Assume whatever you want. You do it anyway." As we used to say, she didn't stutter, utter, or mutter.

In all of this Snoop and Queen never felt the need to fix their face. No facade. No fuckery. They treat their life and business with respect while not giving in to expectations of change or intrusion.

This brings me back to visible hyphens in personal branding. The right one(s) are multi-functional. It can come through in your images. It can be used in your message. It can offer a connection between you and the audience. It can be used to make a point. What it cannot do is compete with all the invisible hyphens you have.

Some people use their families as hyphens. If you're a family brand, that makes sense. If you're a parent who holds your child while designing logos, that makes sense. But, if you're a blunt smoking brother with locs (formerly braids and plaits) who does the Crip walk while using the word nigga at every turn, no one is coming to you for the family experience. That's was the big ass fail when Solo Stove decided to partner with Snoop.

So what is visibly different about Snoop that separates his personal brand from everyone else in the game?

Snoop's Visible Hyphen Boundaries

- Marijuana
- Locs
- Crip walk

Some would call this public image or persona. I see them as brand expansion possibilities. The only one he's currently tapped into is weed, which was no stretch at all. You would be more surprised if he didn't get into the weed gang.

What if Snoop started talking about his hair journey. The time it takes to style before hit'n the business streets. Could you see him starting a hair care line for folx with locs?

You're not a celebrity so let's bring it closer to home. You're a personal branding strategist who drinks bourbon while working, smokes cigars on calls with clients, wears fedoras for podcasting and wear various color reading glasses to compliment what I'm wearing. If you heard that description, who would be top of mind.

Brandma's Visible Hyphen Boundaries

- Fedoras
- Bourbon
- Cigars
- Glasses

Again, public image to some, money makers to a Brandmother. GCB to tap into any one of these markets without breaking a sweat. The new sub-brands would get their credibility from the existing parent brand of the Ghetto Country Brandmother®. The current audience would approve, even though you're not asking their permission, because it's been a part of the brand experience from the beginning.

Breaking into new markets is hard as hell, even for well know brands. Representing them before you attempt to expand diminishes the culture friction between the brand and the audience. You can partner with an existing brand or spin off your own sub-brands, wither way it's a no brainer and win-win for you and the audience.

The advantages to visible hyphens doesn't stop there. As the brand architecture expands, a vibe and culture is built around things that bring you joy. You never have to fix your face for folx who were never gonna buy from you anyway. Your hyphens literally become a statement pieces for conversations that convert.

Using hyphens keeps you from diluting the overall brand

architecture if you're going for a branded house instead of a house of brands. For those that don't know, a branded house is a business structure where all sub-brands operate under one primary brand. It creates a strong, unified brand identity that keeps folx loyal. We're not talking matchy matchy though. Your personal brand hyphens is what ties them all together.

Key elements to GCB's branded house:
- **Core Brand:** Ghetto Country Brandmother®
- Parent/Endorser Brand
- Heart of the brand architecture
- **Business Name:** Brandma's House
- Endorser Brand
- Where offers reside connected to Brandma
- **Audience:** Brandbabies
- Allies, Ambassadors, Advocates
- Feels like fam connected to personal brand
- **Framework:** PB&Slay
- Nurturing solution
- Nourishment coming from Brandma

Benefits to GCB's branded house approach
- **Strong brand recognition:** consistently endorsing Brandma's House using brand specific terms.
- **Fam loyalty:** Brandbabies feel a personal connection to the House

- **Scalability:** new offers can easily fit under the Brandma's House umbrella
- **Consistency:** A core message keeps it clear where the brand stands

That brings us to the look and feel of the sub-brands. Their visuals and vibe take their cues from the personal brand hyphens. First images on the mood board are of you and the things you enjoy. A good graphic designer will make it make sense with subtle nuances for distinction. They'll have a much easier starting point and less revisions because you won't have to try and explain what you want. The brands will be complimentary and aligned throughout the branded house.

To bring it on home, your hyphens provide opportunities storytelling. Unlike a conversation to conversion moment, this is content to conversion. Folx love stories, that's a given. Using your hyphens to tell a story relevant story to what you offer makes your content and marketing further positions your personal brand for top of mind accessibility.

Eight functions from one hyphen.

1. Staying true to self
2. Visual interest
3. Core message connection
4. Audience connection
5. Content pillar
6. Naming offers/services

7. Branching into new markets
8. Relevant storytelling

When you choose to show, and not tell, outside of storytelling, your overall brand architecture benefits. Less stress about relevant content and marketing. This is personal brand positioning on another level. Start with these three questions to choose the hyphens that are right for you.

1. What 3-4 interest/characteristics do I want others to use when describing me and why?

_____

_____

_____

_____

_____

_____

2. How do these interest/characteristics intersect and influence your approach to your work, marketplace, and/or industry?

_____

_____

_____

_____

_____

_____

3. How can you leverage these hyphens to create a more vocal, visible, and vigilant personal brand experience?

_____

_____

_____

_____

_____

_____

The show, not tell quality of visible hyphens are the biggest flex of your personal brand. You position as a niche of one without fixing your face for the masses. Fuck filling gaps. You're not trying to reinvent the wheel. You want to find your happy place for making money.

Using visible hyphens may feel uncomfortable starting out. But the more you own them, the more courageous and confident you become as an authority, expert, and Brand Leader.

Snoop Dogg is one main stream example of how an individual can leverage a named personal brand to expand into other markets. His weed and words are visible hyphens of his interest and characteristics. They set the foundation of his branded house, all things Snoop, not Calvin. By strategically choosing and utilizing your own hyphens, you can achieve Snoop Dogg status.

Your hyphens are a reflection of your true self and thus come through as Brand Ego and Brand Image. Learning to embrace them and flex them to endorse, not pitch, your business just increases your game changer status.

"It's natural. I freestyle, meaning that I just rap. I might put words on paper, but I just put a beat on my rap, and go off the top of my head. It's something I've been able to do for a long time."

- *Snoop Dogg, David Sheff article*

Strengths Are A Set Point

So let's talk about positioning with set points. This is about head space. It's a term used to reference a base line level of a particular psychological state of mind folx return to after a significant life experience. The right set points can continuously bring you back to joy. The wrong ones can stress you the fuck out.

Strengths, like set points, give you what you need to psychological return to the right head space so you maintain your joy. And don't get it twisted. What makes you happy may not be the same thing that brings you joy. Unfortunately, there are more than enough folx willing to lasting joy for momentary happiness? You see it in personal brands that get off on the dopamine high of follows and likes on social media. They replace joy with burn out without compensation.

Reflect back to the hyphens you chose for your personal brand. How many of them actually bring you joy? Whatever ones bring you joy, that makes them a strength. Strengths reinforce your position as an authority.

You have gifts, talents, and abilities that bring you joy. Those are your strengths. There inherent characteristics that have nothing to do with specific roles in your life. Mine is my empathic nature that allows me to pour into people. Yours may be writing fictional stories that create belonging as easily as you blow your nose. Whatever it is, it's enhances the youniqueness of your personal brand.

Snoops talent with words and rhymes were the start of his empire. The enhancement is in how he delivers. His smooth cadence and dialect is distinct. His legendary Crip walk follows him on and off the stage.

He could have easily limited his joy to writing lyrics. Instead he became a rapper. He hasn't dropped a release since 2021, but he will free style in a heart beat. It's how he continues to use and deliver his gift.

Positioning with strength is not a power play, it's about not being easily moved. Movement can be found in your flexibility and adaptability as a Brand Leader. You want to present as distinct, not arrogant. Strengths can be found in the most unlikely of places.

Some strengths are dismissed because they're easy. For some reason we were taught we had to work hard to make money. Heaven forbid you take advantage of a strength because it's too easy. If you think this way, it's why you struggle with pricing.

Remember Snoops other hyphen. Yes, his weed. It brings him joy and he never hid it. He positioned his personal brand as a weed smoker. The only other celebrity I know that openly smokes weed like him is Willie Nelson. Willie's batch is so hard, Toby Keith wrote a song titled, I'll Never Smoke Weed With Willie Again. Well, Snoop was able to capitalize on that even though he never saw it coming.

GCB is planning for what's down the road and has her eye on a bourbon brand. Smoking weed and drinking bourbon are unlikely strengths in every day life. They are brand expansion gold in the business world.

Gifts, talents, and abilities are more acceptable in mainstream business, but so what. You're not in business to be mainstream. Being mainstream is like wearing a sign that says basic and boring. If there is something that gives you joy and doesn't do harm to others, then it could be used as a strength. Haters gonna hate so give 'em something to talk about. That's what leadership is about.

Identifying the right strengths can challenge your comfort zone. And if you didn't hone your gift, talent, or ability for the sake of monetization, it can also make you feel cringy on occasion. That's that pricing problem I mentioned.

It stems from fear and a perception of being misunderstood. Truth is, folx don't want to understand for various reasons. That just means those are not your folx. Or maybe you don't recognize what you do or have as a joy worth sharing. Either way, you end up playing small. And playing small affects your bottom line.

Take parenting for example. Your well meaning parents tell you to ignore your gifts in favor of skills that will fetch a high salary. In their mind, they're doing what's best for you. Out of respect for your parents, you go along. When you grow up you try to recapture what you felt you lost in your youth.

That's mid-life crisis nonsense. It's one of the few times when the saying, "you can't miss what you never had," is bullshit. You always had it, it was just replaced with a money chasing mindset.

Your personal brand is carte blanche to dip into the treasure troves of your youth. Instead of jumping off the cliff of a mid-life cliche, use the most meaningful treasures that bring you joy. Each gem representing something younique and genuine to your being. It doesn't matter that it needs dusting off. Recovering a life of few fucks and fearlessness may not be everyone's cup of tea, so break out the jug and leave them those folx alone.

As you digging through your treasures, don't dump all your shit out for your audience to see. I'm not telling you to hide your mess. I'm say'n be strategic about it. If it doesn't make sense for the personal brand save it for yourself. But you gotta sit in your shit for this one. And if you're still trying to make your parents proud, some guilt will surface. Be okay with that but don't let it be the deciding factor of what goes and what stays.

This is not the time for outside validation and influence. Take away the awards and decorative accolades unless they're a byproduct of what brings you joy. This is a remove the labels and just be yourself kinda strength finder. This is why I always start with contemplation which is the "C" in C.O.D.E. The only question you want to meditate on is, "What do I want?"

Technology makes your life easy as an entrepreneur, but it requires a constant barrage of decisions that seem to fall from the sky like rain. In that world contemplation may seem like a luxury. Yet, it's during that rainstorm that the value of stillness becomes a necessity.

I remember when we were planning to open our first restaurant in downtown Los Angeles. We had partnered with a manager from one the farmers markets where we were vendors. We knew jack all about the process.

Headlines started to appear in the L.A. Times, L.A. Weekly, and other local papers that we were moving downtown. That type of press was one of the reasons they wanted us. My husband and I started feeling pressured to make this happen, but again we were out of our depth.

Me, Neil and Morgan went for our first meeting with Kevin the architect. This was my first time having this type of experience. Talk about out of your comfort zone. He showed us swatches, and photos and how he saw the space. My branding skills weren't what they are now so I just said okay a lot.

The more involved the process got, the less we saw The Manager. When Kevin came back with the renders for what was supposed to be our new place they were boughie and beautiful. Big dark wood beams. A wall made of firewood. Open pit facing the customers. Red domed pendent lighting hanging over heavy wooden high tables from vaulted ceilings. As amazing as it was it didn't fit our brand, but all we said was okay.

Then came the general contractor. We're paying for plans and permits and dishing out money like ballers. But at home Neil and I were lost because The Manager gave us the impression that he was covering the build out. When we questioned him about it, his whole spiel changed.

Before we signed anymore documents we had a come to Jesus talk. We were looking at a five year lease with a hefty triple net. The build out that was gonna cost over $200,000. The deposit on the architectural plans was $8,000. We were already outta pocket for over $20,000. So during our conversation we had to contemplate and ask ourselves, "What do we really want?"

We didn't want to drive from Long Beach to downtown L.A. everyday at 3am only to fight traffic for an hour and a half to get back home. We wanted more of a hole in the wall spot for locals, than a boughie place for boughie folx.

We made our decision and walked away from it all $20,000 poorer. We found an old pizza shop in Long Beach and bought the business for the assets. No fuss no muss. We did the same for our second location.

We were able to continue capitalizing on our strengths of hospitality that we were raised with. The same strengths that got us headlines. The same strengths that got us on Man Fire Food and The Great Food Truck Race. And I didn't fix my face for any of it.

Strengths are not a learned skill but it can be a practiced gift, talent or ability. If everything that surfaces during your contemplation of strengths includes superficial and material shit, I suggest you go down the rabbit hole of why. Once you reach the bottom of why you want that strength, you may change your answer.

The gems of joy you find will be refined into jewels for the personal brand. Like me, you might find joy in mellowing out with a cigar and bourbon. But the key isn't the specific activity itself; it's the aspect associated with it that brings joy. In my case, it's the ritual of unwinding and appreciating good company. GCB embodies this by creating a space in Brandma's' House where folx from different backgrounds, cultures, and ethnicities, can connect over shared experiences, not just cigars and bourbon.

Refining gems into jewels for your personal brand is about a focus of joyful strength. Everyone's not gonna appreciate the brilliance of it, and that's okay. It's like putting together a guest list for THE perfect party. You invite folx whom you have a mutual appreciation with. The party stays pop'n because of the invitees connection to you. Your personal brand is your party, and the gems you refine are the conversation pieces that attract them.

Those same strengths can now be used to make you distinctively more visible. Your platform of choice becomes your party venue. You can choose social media, posting a blog, or podcasting. The entertainment comes through in the content you produce. Knowing your gift for writing, talking, or being visible is another strength.

You can be exclusive by choosing only one platform or you can be a socialite by showing up everywhere. Contemplate where and how you strengths can be most brilliant. Do you see yourself kill'n it by being engaging on social media? Or maybe a blog lets you go deep in the game of your expertise? Maybe you're a talker and a podcast is calling to you? Each platform offers unique strength value, so choose what works best for where you are now.

Knowing your natural gifts – whether it's a talent for writing engaging articles, delivering thought-provoking talks, or captivating viewers with video – leverage it. Embrace that thing instead of struggling with tricks and trends. This is not only consistently easy, it showcases the brilliance of your jewels to attract a larger audience.

1. What are the things that you do for yourself by yourself that bring you the most joy in life and why?

_____

_____

_____

_____

_____

2. What comes so easy to you that it makes you think everyone else is dumb for thinking it's so hard?

_____

_____

_____

_____

_____

3. What energizes you to the point that someone has to come in and stop you?

_____

_____

_____

_____

_____

This is your set point of positioning. It's your magic, your fairy dust, your very own MC Hammer, Can't Touch This, kinda shit. Fusing your hyphens with your strengths your roots for standing ten toes down. It's establishing boundaries so folx have no choice but to come through the only entry you leave open. You're a better alternative to others in the same game because they're clear about that.

If you're into fleeting trends and popularity contest, then you know this is not for you. This is about a space only you can occupy, a nice of one, built on your "ten toes down" commitment to being true to you. It's a personal brand that makes you exceptional because it embraces a paradox of beauty that's real and relatable for some and repellant to others.

This is your space and you're building an empire around it. Folx will be drawn to its brilliance and celebrate it. Haters are gonna do what haters do. That's a problem reserved specifically for them. Their hateration is background noise compared to the harmonious connection with your target audience.

"So don't blame me for the problems. You can't fault me for it. You can't blame me. You want to blame me but I'm just trying to express what is going on, and trying to keep America open to it."

- *Snoop Dogg, David Sheff article*

Language Is A Landmark

I'm bad at remembering street names but I know my landmarks. Consider that a landmark is more than a spot on your gps. It's a beacon, a reference point, a tangible marker. It defines, delineates, and declares that a space is occupied.

Language is your landmark boundary. Every word you use, every turn of phrase, is a boundary of separation. And just as a physical landmark can change the lay of the land, your language can change the perception of your personal brand.

Consider the impact of your words when you speak or write in a language younique to your personal brand. It can be a one word mashup like Brandma, that encompasses the essence of the overall brand. Or it could be as subtle as your constant action verb of transformation. How ever you string them together you use your words to connect the offer and the audience.

I talk a lotta shit by some folx standard. But instead of scrolling or strolling past me, they themselves end up talking shit. I'm okay with that just don't be disrespectful. You can speak to me but you can't speak about me to me.

Having a strong opinion is not a problem. But if it's doesn't lead to a landmark conversation of conversion then it's wasted words. It's when you have no opinion but talk shit anyway that your words become meaningless to the audience. You have a communication issue. But before you can even fix that issue, you gotta fix your language issue.

Establishing language as the final reinforcement of your personal brand position shapes your territory for inbound marketing. Using your words to speak the language of the audience isn't as crazy as it sounds. It's all about the lifecycle stages of inbound marketing.

The cycle begins when someone new finds you via socials. Your language makes them curious and maybe a bit uncomfortable because it's not the okie doke they were expecting. They see your personal brand as an anomaly, so they're not sure if you're talking shit or drop'n gems. This is the brand awareness stage where the trifecta of your hyphens, strengths and language will hit hardest.

The next stage in the cycle happens when they keep coming back. Eventually, the follow you back to your site and give you their email. They're starting to feel like they understand you. And they like that you're not talking like everyone else. It's not how they would say it, but then they "never thought of it that way." This is consideration stage and they're parroting your language because they're being nurtured.

Then finally they are all in and they recognize the landmark language. Everything they read sounds like you're reading to them. When they use one of your key phrases, you're top of mind. Whether they spend money with you or not, they are now at the loyalty stage. They will either become a client or send you referrals without ever purchasing.

You can ask AI to help you with language but it will never be able to speak your language. Something will always be a bit off. It can put words in place to mimic you or the tone you prompt. That is not the same thing. The language your personal brand uses to communicate with your audience is a blend influenced by heritage, culture, and expertise. What the words mean to your brand is lost on AI

If you've had formal training in your area of expertise, you know the jargon. If you're like me and learned the hard way before you got formal training, you may ignore a lot of the jargon. The thing that's missing from your audience is their influence on the language. Unless you're trying to attract folx JUST LIKE YOU, you have to learn to speak their language using your words. Sounds weird, I know.

Learning a new language is hard. So when someone comes across your content and you don't sound like everyone else in your industry, they have to learn a new language. To make it easier you use your words to speak their language. A great way to do this is to use archetypes.

Ghetto Country Brandmother® has an archetype mix of Rebel/Caregiver:

Communication Style: Assertive

Influence: Parental Dichotomy

Language: Tough Brand Love

Tone: Bossy Mom Vibe

Bold Brandbabies are independent individuals who are curious and courageous. They have are not content with staying put so they color outside the lines of conventionalism. They also have a rebellious streak because they're strongly self-aware. So how does Brandma use her words to speak their language?

Here are some headlines I found on LinkedIn of folx who call themselves "personal brand strategist."

Samples:

- **Everyone else:** I empower you to be your authentic self
- **Everyone else:** Elevate your brand with the power of image
- **Everyone else:** Get visible and grow your industry authority
- **Brandma:** Certified 💯 empathic bitch nurturing the personal life, brand, & business of Founder Brandbabies who want to grow, scale, & expand

I believe in branding by example and language is a part of that. It's language to scare away the crybabies and attract the troublemakers and outcast. The content language that follows doesn't fit the algorithm norm so I'm not one of the popular kids. That means who ever rolls with me on the regular is pick'n up what I'm put'n down.

Using your archetypal language mashup to paint a picture instead of describe becomes a love language between you and the audience. It expands the brand vocabulary, vernacular, and verbiage.

This is not one of my alliteration tangents. This is your personal brand being expressive when an expert opinion is warranted. Look at Snoop. He reps the culture of the LBC and blackness. His three V's are expressed mostly through his rap. He continues to use the language of the streets even as he matured out of them. Let's break it down and explore a bit more.

Language is one of the most nuanced things about communication. Even sign language can be distinguished by region. Whether it's your dialect or accent, somebody get's you or wants to because of how you speak. Language is all about words, sentence structure, and linguistic nuance whether it's spoken or written. I mentioned AI before and as much as they teach it, it loses something in the translation.

Snoop and Martha have an exclusive language that a lotta folx don't understand so they stand on the outside making assumptions about their friendship. Growing up we would've called Snoop a sell out for hanging with someone like Martha. Folx ignore the fact that his friendship has allowed him to expand into other markets that would have seemed strange to him before. There common language is business. The loss of a language barrier opens doors.

Since you don't currently have the reach, riches, or recognition of Snoop Dogg or Martha Stewart you need a language that's speaks to more than one other person. You need a language that speaks to an audience that doesn't require translation. The language barrier that may be between you now can come down if you teach them your language and help them understand it.

This is not to be confused with dragging out industry jargon.

I try not to use big brands to make a point but here's an exception. "Just do it." A simple phrase that crosses language barriers. It belongs to Nike but it crosses so many areas of life. Whenever someone says it, everyone in the room consciously or sub-consciously thinks of Nike.

I don't remember the first time I heard about love languages, but it's a real thing. And while business with big budgets pay for data on how to get a hook into the audience, you can do the same thing with a language landmarks throughout your content. Find the right words for those you want to attract and develop your language.

Only when you develop a shared language does communication truly begin to happen. It removes the stigma's of feeling excluded for some while others exclude themselves. And thus you transform a barrier into a boundary. It doesn't clear the way for everyone, just the right ones. It emotes for the brand and provides clarity for the audience.

You have problems with clarity when the audience doesn't understand the context. Phrases, taglines, and lexicons are repeatable because they hold meaning for the person saying them. It's the context of words being literal and/or figurative.

Did you notice the phrase, ten toes down, being repeated throughout the book. I heard that from someone who got it from someone else. And when you think about it, the literal meaning of ten toes down doesn't make sense. But from a figurative sense of being deeply rooted in beliefs and convictions, it makes total sense. If someone wants to fight you on either level, to engage is to waste your time. Defensive language has its place but it's not a go to for clarity.

Which takes me to the next point of words having value. I was raised to believe that what comes out of your mouth comes from your heart. It's based on a bible scripture. Another bible scripture talks about the power of life and death is in the power of the tongue. I'm not bible thump'n but it's a thing. Think of how often the right words pushed you over the edge into something good or bad? How often do you wish you could catch the words in mid air? You meant what you said but you didn't mean to say them out loud.

"Professional" language will have you tip toeing around issues that are near and dear to your brand values. It's an avoidance of emotional connection. Why would you do that? Being vocal about the right things, not everything, makes shit echo throughout your branded house.

Disconnecting from the emotion allows you to treat your audience like data and reduce them to numbers. It's like removing all the nutrients from food then selling it back to you as a supplement. Being a role model for emotional connection makes big brands nervous. They have a persona, you have a person.

The language of your personal brand can go where advertising can't. It's the language boundary that strengthens your position. The only way big brands can respond is that they have to pay to play. By that I mean advertise as a way to dampen the voices of personal brands.

The landmark language of your personal brand is a literal and figurative connection between your offer and your audience. Strengthening it can affect equity and pricing. What you say, how you say it, when you say it provides the clarity and emotion of the core message. The literal sense behind your words form the foundation of the message, while the figurative meaning adds depth and emotion, creating a richer brand experience.

1. What specific words or phrases do you want to be associated with your personal brand, and why do you believe they'll resonate?

_____

_____

_____

_____

_____

2. How do you think altering your language tone or style could better align with your communication style?

_____

_____

_____

_____

_____

3. How can you use feedback or recurring themes from your audience's responses to refine your language and lexicons?

_____

_____

_____

_____

_____

Just like Snoop and Martha, who transcend origins and up-bringing to develop a language for two, your personal brand can turn barriers into boundaries through a landmark language for two, you and the audience. No jargon or impressive words needed. It's the ten toes down effect of your beliefs and convictions in a game of show, not tell.

Remember, the right words have the power to inspire, motivate, and transform. I can be a literal asshole when it comes to words and definitions. But creating a shared understanding goes beyond literal interpretation, allowing your audience to feel seen and understood. Developing the boundaries of your personal brand is removing language barriers for those who want to take you up on your offer.

In the end, your language becomes a mix tape of heritage, culture, education, experience, and expertise. It is a living, evolving expression of your growth as a brand leader. Embrace it, refine it, and use it to maintain the boundaries of your personal brand. Speaking with clarity and conviction not only allows your message to knock down barriers, it creates lasting impression.

"A lot of brands, you can't touch them. When you're dealing with Snoop Dogg, he brings you closer to the brand and it feels like it's a part of you."

- *Snoop Dogg, Forbes*

BROADCASTING

I remember when people who were on the radio and the news were called broadcasters. They would dispense information with nothing more than a matter of fact voice of facts and figures. The evolution from broadcaster to anchor person, television personality, or entertainment host seems so far removed from just providing information.

We're in an era where most of what you want to know is a click away, and yet the validity of the information is called into question by anyone with a cell phone and opposing opinion. That makes everyone a broadcaster now. You can talk on any topic you want and draw an audience.

So why are so many founders silent? Caught in a trick bag of self-doubt and insecurities. Relying on information that has no basis in truth has been the death of a lot of great ideas.

Don't Be So Damn Loud

My first crush was a Main Street Mafia. But my first love was a drug dealer sling'n rocks on the ho stroll of 108th & Fig. This was back in the early 80's. We were just two broken kids who found each other from a wrong number.

By night he would stand on the corner in his creased jeans, crisp white tee, and blue corduroy slippers with a beanie pulled low on his head. By day he was a top student in a private school who had acceptance letters from various colleges. But college was not for him.

It wasn't that, let's call him A, didn't want to go to college. It was that he had to sell enough crack to get his mom away from his abusive father. And by the time he did that he was so far down the rabbit hole of that life, there was no exit.

One year A bought me a fuchsia colored BMW with yellow, orange, and red racing strips. I loved that car. Whenever I left my apartment in Leimert Park, I would open my sunroom, turn up my radio and make the world take notice. And boy did they notice.

Since we moved around a lot when I was younger my stomping ground was big. Plus I had family all around L.A. Well on day I was out doing errands and was about to get in my car when someone stopped and asked me, "Aren't you A's girl?"

I politely said, "Excuse me?"

"Aren't you A's girl? I recognize the car."

A and I lived two different lifestyles that seldom bumped into each other, despite us spending so much time together. But in that deer in the headlights moment I was scared. Instantly I saw myself as a dope dealers girl, riding around in an unmistakable target. How many other folx had associated my joy ride'n ass with A?

For months I drove my car like it didn't matter where it came from. I knew his crew knew, but they were fam and only one of them had ever ventured from 108th with A to my apartment in Leimert Park. And just that quick, the joy of my car was gone because I had broadcasted that I was a dope dealers girl?

When folx are having a good time, loud is a given. Or is that just me? Toning that shit down for the sake of being "professional" was hard because I knew where I was from. I have one of those "voices that carry," as they say. Great for choir singing, not so much for corporate speak.

I'm no stranger to using an inside voice, but not everything is meant to be done quietly. You gotta make some noise to get some attention. But what you want is the right attention. And if that's the case, you should have fun doing it.

I spend most of my time on LinkedIn for content marketing purposes. What I see when I post there are folx from every kinda industry giving advice on personal branding. It's not even remotely near their lane, and yet they feel qualified to offer advice based on "they're" personal brand.

There's also those who consider themselves personal branding experts for "LinkedIn." All they talk about is visibility on LinkedIn. Update your profile on LinkedIn. Use a professional photo on LinkedIn. They're depending on folx trying to market on that one platform.

Sadly, most of this expert advice is about self-promotion. If you're trying to stay self-employed, then by all means, promote yourself. Folx who go overboard with it end up building an audience of folx making self-promoting comments. Those aren't leads. Making it all about you leaves little room for them. And anyone who is interested is gonna go straight for the price comparison because you're like every other self-promoter.

If branding leads to marketing then your personal brand should be marketing as an endorser broadcasting a core message mixed with value and stories. The only part that's about you is how you want to get it done. Learning to be a broadcaster is not for the ego driven.

There's a big difference between broadcasting like a dope dealers girlfriend and providing useful information. That's what broadcasting is you know? Sending out information to a lotta folx who are willing to pay attention. I know that sounds condescending but it's not. It's that so many terms are ignored or misused that I want to be clear.

When you shout to get attention, folx fear you. But when

you shout to give information, folx wanna be near you. Shifting from self-promotion to endorsement is a challenge for folx with big egos. It fits the I am my brand spectacle. Everyone needs to know, you put in the work, you did the design, you were in a magazine. This combined with charge your worth is why some folx struggle as entrepreneurs.

The broadcasting of a message based on self-worth for self-promotion is not marketing. By all means, be proud of your accomplishments and accolades, but stop believing that's where your core message resides.

This is about your money and only a select few are gonna come outta pocket when you're shouting look at me. You're positioning yourself as the solution instead of separating yourself from it. That positions says, no one is ever good enough to replace you. And so you hinder the growth of your business.

Broadcasting via advertising seems easy. Your ROI says different. Paid self-promotion is still self-promotion. That's because throwing money at a situation is easy, even for broke folx. It's a one to many approach that doesn't fix your broadcasting problem.

So how do you broadcast with a personal brand? How do you broadcast about something you've put so much into without positioning yourself as the solution? A product can sell itself, but a service, that's a different ball of wax. You made it for them so it can't be about you. When it's time to put a price on it, you either "charge your worth" or fail to sell because you don't know your worth.

Oh, I can feel the cringe creeping up my neck.

In the early days of working the farmers market, to attract the crowd Neil would yell...

"BARBECUE! BARBECUE! BARBECUE!"

It was as easy as breathing for him. He didn't yell at the top of his voice but it carried far enough throughout the market to get attention. For a long time I felt a sense of embarrassment. Somehow in my mixed up head it felt like we were begging folx to buy from us. I preferred the, if you build it they will come, plan of action. It didn't matter that deep down I knew that was the dumbest shit ever.

If not for Neil's broadcasting abilities I'm not sure how much barbecue we wouldn't have sold. But not every personality is suited for that type of loud and proud messaging. For me it was the lingering effect of chastisement about my loudness. Instead of owning it, I tried to hide it and hated when it would seep out. I equated my loudness with my bigness (technically, tallness). The so called harmless jokes from family left a lasting impression that makes me self-conscious to this day. Some would consider me stigmatized by my experience. I just say, it is what it is.

Enter social media and an influx of side hustles, influencers, and content creators. The word on the street was that you had to market yourself or self-promote. Talk about traumatizing. Like most, I appreciate being heard, valued, and recognized for my contributions. However, I do not crave the spotlight unless I'm speaking to an audience.

Transitioning from self-promoter to endorser made inbound marketing easier. It's about shift the focus from you to the business. Endorse your own shit, the results, the clients, the framework. It's an almost imperceptible flex of your gifts, talents, and abilities. And you do it with a promise the business can keep.

That's right! Your personal brand becomes an endorser brand. That's more inline with inbound marketing principles. Endorser branding is strategic and it cultivates long-term client relationships.

Being an endorser brand is not the same as getting an endorsement deal with athletes and celebrities. Nor should it be compared to influencers who get brand deals. Endorser brands **own** all of the sub-brands it endorses. The sub-brands in turn leverages the reputation and recognition of the endorser brand for greater credibility.

Another name for endorser brands is parent brand. Seems fitting for a brandmother, but that's not the point. Using Snoop as the example, his personal brand as Snoop Dogg is the parent brand for every sub-brand associated with it. The owner of all of it is Calvin Broadus, Jr. In that respect he's like Richard Branson who owns the Virgin brand. Virgin Group is the endorser (parent) brand of over 400 sub-brands.

As an endorser brand, Virgin can stand on its own. Richard doesn't need to be an endorser brand for anything Virgin. Snoop, however, is hands on as an endorser brand. Media always refers to him as Snoop Dogg and not Calvin Broadus, Jr.

Imagine broadcasting as an endorser brand and the valuable information you share is about everything you own. And because you're such a credible broadcaster, the value of your endorsement extends to your offers. This is not about yammering, announcing, and publicizing you as a brand. This is your personal brand endorsing with **youniqueness**, **amplification**, and **projection**.

Folx will tell you to shut your Y.A.P. just because on social media. They're not your business. It's your business to broadcast a younique perspective within your industry. You then need to amplify that broadcast so it projects across the audience.

As the endorser brand, Y.A.P.ing is a strategic level up to the game. It's an investment in the long-term success of your brand architecture. You're positioned at the top of the inbound marketing funnel attracting folx who are lookin for a real person with a real solution. This is where the money resides for life-long clients.

The broadcasting endorser brands name and/or other identifiers are aligned in some shape, form, or fashion to the sub-brands. It's not something you normally see with personal branding. Snoop, Oprah, and Gary Vee are a few of the exceptions. But again, Oprah and Gary turned their personal names into brands which is different than a named personal brand like Snoop.

Personal brands as endorsers outweigh the message in a bottle effect of a business brand persona imitation for advertising purposes. But when you only broadcast about yourself (market yourself), then it can never be about the audience. And if you can't make it about them, then they don't give a shit about you.

An audience is more inclined to connect with a person than a persona. Personal brands genuinely engage with the audience, offers an occasional flex that's attractive, and reinforces the promise made by the value proposition. It's something an audience wants to tune into, not tune out.

Your broadcast is part of the overall brand experience. Say it long enough and loud enough, eventually it's as recognizable as a logo and as distinctive as a fingerprint. It's amplified by the audience and clients swear by it.

Broadcasters are positioned to lead the world by controlling the narrative. They put a familiar face on harsh realities. The era of impersonal corporate brands is fading. And with AI all the rage, folx are craving a real connection. Personal brands as endorsers are the future of growing, scaling, and expanding businesses.

The noise and nonsense of self-promotion is growing out real voices. Stop with the egotistical trap of entrepreneurship and embrace the endorsement of it.

"You got to be
who you are when you are."

- *Snoop Dogg*

Yammering Is Not Younique

Back in the day we used to call folx out for "selling wolf tickets." It meant that your mouth was writing a check your ass couldn't cash. If you kept talk'n then somebody might start throw'n hay makers. Oh god I'm so fucking old.

Anyway, let's reduce wolf tickets to yammering. You still talking a whole lotta shit but it's not gonna getcha assed whooped. In a world where every entrepreneur has a smart phone, you can't escape the yammering but you do ignore most of it. That's because yammering is like white noise for folx on the scroll.

Broadcast endorsers don't position with yammering. They position with youniqueness. It's a combination of your hyphens, strengths, and language. Alone they're nothing special. Put together as part of a personal brand and they position you as a niche of one. This is cool if you don't fall victim to inner yammering. That shit comes through loud and clear.

Inner yammering can make you see yourself side ways. And how you see yourself is more important than how others see you. How you talk to yourself about yourself is twice as important. When all you speak are fears and anxiety to yourself, then any message you broadcast will come across as weak.

Your core message is met with disinterest and nonchalance.

You're attempting to endorse your business and you don't even believe the words that are coming out of your mouth. You fear you have no youniqueness. That because you think you have to make your business about you and that makes you uncomfortable.

The constant low-grade hum of self-promoting bullshit seeps in and subliminally encourages your inner hater to speak up. Everyone has a personal brand peddling their "unique" brand of bullshit. It's a barrage of listed hyphens and hype. But because they the squeaky wheel gets the oil, you think they're broadcast is best. They're still listing their hyphens and hyping themselves. That's not endorser broadcasting.

Youniqueness positioning is not loud or flashy. It's genuine and relatable. The audience listens to you because you found a way to say the same shit that allow them to see it through your lens. The mix and blend of hyphens you can see, strengths that are brilliant, and a love language they want to learn, makes you all the things. Think of the remix as a reinforced tower from which to broadcast.

Inner yammering is why you need courage, not ego. Stopping that noise is what the reinforcement trinity is all about. Only you can own how those pieces come together to form the youniqueness of your broadcaster. You may never kill the inner yammering but you can beat it down a lot with belief in self and what you bring to the game.

Remember, you gave birth to a business. If you listen to

the inner yammering about your worth, that doubt will spill over into every aspect of your empire. Contemplation leads to self-awareness, in understanding the TRUTH about your gifts, talents, and abilities.

This is your game to play and you have to play to win, not just sit in. You don't have to announce you're the winner because. How you broadcast the game will put everyone on notice.

If you forget how to talk to yourself with love and encouragement, fear will rule your attempt at entrepreneurship. Giving voice to those fears in the wrong context is not a sign of vulnerability, but of a train wreck waiting to happen.

As mature as you are, you're never far removed from that scared kid in school feeling. That kid who wants to fit in and be liked. It's compounded by the seeds your protective parents planted in an effort to save you from being teased or bullied. It feeds the self-talk that hinders your youniqueness.

Youniqueness requires you to be courageous enough to take ownership of you. When no one else will stand ten toes down for you. It's easy to live life on your terms when no one's looking. But when folx start to take notice, you chip away bits of your youniqueness so you're not seen as an outsider. You cower in the face of expectations and acceptable societal norms.

With all the labels and roles of life, folx get their panties in a twist when you use a label to position your personal brand in a way that doesn't fit their narrative. It fucks with their sensibilities and paradigm of the world. It's all about the Expectancy

Violation Theory and that has nothing to do with you. It's not your responsibility.

Expectancy violation theory (EVT) is basically how folx respond when someone does something outside their expectations. It's like when I call myself professional and folx clutch their pearls when I use profanity. But here's the good part. It can bad as well as good. Either way, it works in favor of the broadcast and your youniqueness.

The expectancy violation of your personal brands younique broadcast is a good thing for folx who are tired of the okie doke. Again, my big brand example is Apple when they launched the first iPhone. They violated exceptions in a good way. So depending on the situation, you can make it work in your favor.

Deliberate violations put your personal brand on the offensive, not defensive. It's a strategic and intentional way to broadcast that doesn't lead to yammering. When things don't go as planned, you're prepared, adaptable, and responsive. If you're turning to many folx off then you fix your shit accordingly.

Expectancy violation is not about being shocking for shock sakes. It's about understanding how folx react to your youniqueness. If you're cool with it and they aren't, then you may have to adjust your messaging, pricing, or chosen platform.

EVT is why folx use words like accommodate, assimilate, and acclimate. Their attempt at being distinct is to wear a spotted tie when everyone else wears stripes. Or they add a vibrant streak of color to their hare. They're tip toe around the fringes of expectancy violence. Their personal brand is positioned as similar to others in the industry. In turn it makes no difference what broadcast you listen to.

So instead of developing a personal brand that conforms to these terms, flip the script and get your audience to accommodate, assimilate, and acclimate to your broadcast. As I write this I see the love hate relationship folx are having with Snoop at the Olympics in Paris. He brought his Uncle Snoop A-game and folx are loving him, but. But he's a pot head. But he promotes drug use.

Despite all the butts, Snoop hasn't missed a beat. Only thing he did was put his blunt game on the back burner. He didn't change the broadcast. He adapted to respect the rules of someone else's playing field and take advantage of an opportunity. He's earned the credibility to broadcast on his terms. Other's wish they could but instead they play the role of bitter bitches.

So back to you. You chose the thug life of entrepreneurship and that requires business and brand leadership. And as the leader your core job description is in the title role. Lead folx so you close the gap between the offer and the audience.

So don't go out like a sucka duck. Be an endorser brand with a younique boundary mix of hyphens, strengths, and language. That's the position of someone with a message worth listening to. It is the courage, if not confidence, of hyphens, strengths, and language that get's you past that initial awkwardness of broadcasting.

Youniqueness of personal branding is not on the same level as the uniqueness of a personal life. You have infinite possibilities in your personal life. You have intentional possibilities in your personal brand. To get that level of clarity you gotta leave some bullshit at the door.

I want you to think about who you are when you spend money vs. who you are when you make money. If they seem the same to you then you're projecting, not broadcasting. This affects the impact of your marketing and your bottom line.

The uniqueness of your personal life is based on the paradigm of how you live. It determines how you spend your time. The youniqueness of your personal brand is based on paradigm of how you generate revenue. It determines the value of your time.

Using your personal life as a brand to generate revenue is a projection. You're using it to tell folx how you wanna live and asking them to foot the bill. And even though you gain a big following, no one wants to pay you to live a life they don't have or want. You go for the projection because you think it's easy and makes you seem relatable. In actuality, you're afraid to lead so you hide behind your life.

You can stop hiding if you own your hyphens, strengths, and language. However you mix or mash them up, it's still you, just not all of you. That is the youniqueness you bring to the money game. It is what you need when it's time to broadcast in a way that gets you seen and paid. "But what about competitors?" What about them?

Marketers who are chasing corporate dollars are the ones worried about competition. And no matter how much you try to duck and dodge them, their ads find you. Big business wants to stay top of mind and they have a lotta money to make that happen. You do not. Plus you can't compete with them, or any other founder out there, anymore than you can compete with your gardener and his loud ass mower when you're on a zoom call. So stop.

Competition has its place but personal branding is not it. The youniqueness of your personal brand broadcasting a message via social media is great for inbound marketing. No one can compete with a niche of one because only you are youniquely qualified to play this game.

Baby, you gotta stop let'n folx push you into learned helplessness. Yes, the thug life of entrepreneurship comes at a cost. But you're not responsible for folx who ain't cool with how your personal brand gets down. It's a matter of respectful rebellion all up and through.

TOP FIVE

Hyphens	Strengths	Language
_____	_____	_____
_____	_____	_____
_____	_____	_____
_____	_____	_____
_____	_____	_____

TOP THREE

Hyphens	Strengths	Language
_____	_____	_____
_____	_____	_____
_____	_____	_____

Describe Your Youniqueness:
mix & mash til it works

1st Draft: _____

_____

_____

_____

_____

2nd Draft: _____

_____

_____

_____

_____

3rd Draft: _____

_____

_____

_____

_____

Youniqueness is not about perfection. It's about the fit of the personal brand. It's how you make your money. It may be a bit uncomfortable at first, like breaking in new shoes. But if you feel like you're gonna fall on your face, then it doesn't fit.

Once you find that fit, it's easier to get the word out. The message you broadcast to the audience will be genuine and younique. And your comfort will come across as confidence.

You can stop the yammering and get to the point of making money where you stand.

"I went out and got little jobs. I was selling candy as a teenager, selling newspapers. But as I got older, I didn't want to sell that anymore. I wanted to make more money."

- Snoop Dogg

Amplify For The ATM

You crave attention for your brand. Attention is why babies cries, toddlers throw tantrums, and Karen's lose their shit. It's a primal urge to be seen, heard and valued. But the world where brand equity resides is overrun with yammering folx who "are brands." Getting caught in that trap yourself leads you to believe louder is better.

Personal branding loudness comes in the form of vanity metrics called followers. So folx sell you on getting more followers, not necessarily the right followers, but followers nonetheless. So get loud and the world will listen. Right!

WRONG!

Being loud is easy, speaking as a naturally loud person. But to be impactful and influential, you gotta be more than loud. You can just go around telling everyone you're authentic. You gotta come with your own amplifier.

Amplification doesn't require you to be loud because it puts a mic in your hand. It's how your broadcast carries further and with clarity. It's an art that makes your voice resonate, not echo. No need to try and drown out the so-called competition because you're harmonizing with the audience.

Amplification is like good gumbo. Being loud is like you throwing seafood in water, hoping it will make a good pot of gumbo.

Amplification on the other hand, is putting in work for the gumbo. It's about understanding the roux, the seasonings, and the simmer your broadcast needs.

Going from loud to amplified requires a position transition. You have peel off the need for personal validation through loudness and get suited and booted to amplify for resonance. Broadcasting with a younique voice and finding the right platform is where you start to amplify.

Let's shift for a minute. When I first heard the phrase, available target market (ATM), it sent me down a rabbit hole. While I was down there, I kept hearing the phrase, where the money resides where the money resides. At some point I hit digital currency and connected the dots. But before I get too deep, I wanna paint an ugly picture for you.

I often refer to branding as a pimp game. Folx don't like it because they get caught up on the semantics. How is it wrong when the word on the street is that, you're a brand and you should market yourself? It's bad advice doled out, like candy from a stranger, by the self-employed freelancers and solopreneurs. Personally, I have no problem with the pimp game if everyone is a consenting adult not harming others. But when you lie about being a ho while doing ho shit. I have no respect for that.

Now in this pimp game of marketing yourself, there are those at the low end and those at the high end. Folx at the high-end thinks the CEO and c-suite folx are their ideal client so they keep yelling at him to get attention. Folx at the low end don't have an ideal client so they keep yammering. And no matter how much they yell and yammer folx aren't listening.

There used to be a saying that you don't pay a trick for "services" you pay them to leave. Well, you're not getting paid for either. You're just being loud. Are you still with me or are you rushing to give me a bad review on Amazon.

Instead of yelling at the ideal client, amplify for the ideal audience they reside in. Everyone is trying to get the ideal clients attention with cheap tricks. The message is loud but weak. All you're attracting are the broke folx trying to make a dollar outta fifteen cents. Those are the folx who want the quick and dirty tricks you offer up for free.

This could be a messaging issue, but what if it's not? Amplifying for an ATM instead of yelling for an ideal client is where the money resides. It's all in the positioning of the broadcast.

Everywhere you turn someone is asking you about your ideal client. You know, that imaginary unicorn you made up, gave a name, and slapped a face on. Close your eyes and try to picture that unicorn waiting for you to show up. Do you see 'em? Can you pick 'em out of a line up?

Oh wait. There is no line up because that would be to easy and social media don't make it easy. So shift your gaze from the unicorn. There's a herd of wild horses you looked past to see the unicorn. You ignored them so they ignored you. But in that herd is a unicorn in disguise because they're tired of being yelled at.

Attracting an ATM of wild horses is better than doing tricks for price shoppers and content carnivores disguised as unicorns. Amplifying your broadcast for an ATM with similar funds, functions, and fondness means you don't have to get loud because they're plentiful and accessible. Your youniqueness (hyphens, strengths, and language) provides the landscape for them to show up. That's how your broadcast taps into the biases.

Bias in branding and marketing is considered taboo. Or so I've been told. I call bullshit because if you're broadcasting a message based on shared values, opinions and the like, then bias is all up and through. Oh, maybe they just don't want to call a thing a thing. But that's not your problem.

In the real world, ideal clients are those who pay their invoices on time, don't complain about the work, and advocate for your business. Getting them to reveal themselves through heuristic bias is the game changer especially since you don't have to fix your face.

PSA: Don't use bias as an excuse to be an asshole

The art of broadcasting a heuristically biased message is found in the original boundaries of your personal brand DNA: Contemplation, Objectives, Dedication, and Ethics (C.O.D.E.). It's the premise of your core message. By intentionally tapping into heuristic bias, the mental shortcut for making decisions simpler, you deepen the position of your personal brand.

Repeated exposure to an amplified biased broadcast reinforces the impact. It gets in the head of your audience and takes root like a favorite song. In order to leverage the repetition, you have to vary the delivery and maintain the conviction. If you get lazy, stagnant, and trendy, they'll become desensitized and you'll run them off. So let's get into the biases.

1. Affect Bias

Affect is a verb that refers to influence. In the context of heuristics, it's about how emotions influence judgement. So as much as folx try to fight it, their decision-making is influenced by emotion first, then logic. The message you broadcast is limited information for the audience. In a nutshell that's marketing. The audience then has to make a decision of what to do with that information. If it has no emotional value, then a decision is made to keep it push'n. This is why folx keep telling you, you have three seconds to get their attention. The oldest part of your brain can process an emotion quicker than you can yell.

2. Framing Bias

Framing the message of your broadcast can be linked to language, tone, words, and inflections. So what you say and how you say it with your personal brand sends indicators about your overall brand architecture. You can frame whether it's high-end or low rent without ever using the words like luxury or premium. Framing can position your brand architecture as a solution without rattling off your list of intangible hyphens.

3. Anchoring Bias

What you see is what you can be the ultimate anchor bias of first impressions. It can be as blatant as skin color or as subtle as colorful eyewear. The hyphens from boundaries can enhance the anchor bias in your favor. If it doesn't that will make it a last impression. It can put you top of mind as high-end or low rent. Broadcasting a message with a personal brand can provide an anchor that your website copy cannot. Attaching a face to the overall brand establishes a deeper connection. And since the anchor encounter helps them make a quick decision, once logic catches up with emotion, they're gonna spend money with you.

4. Representation Bias

Folx would rather you represent the stereotype in their heads to be comfortable. But personal branding is not about fitting a stereotype. It's about being top of mind. That's why your boundaries are so important. Instead of stereotype, a personal brand can use an archetype mix. Ghetto Country Brandmother® is an archetype mix of caregiver and rebel. An archetype mix combined with the established hyphen, strength and language boundaries, offers a distinct and consistent representation for the personal brand.

5. Availability Bias

If anchoring can put you top of mind with a first impression, availability can keep you there. This is about visibility and value-based content. No trend or algorithm chasing. If you write, write a post, article, or ebook at regularly scheduled intervals. If you're a talker, then podcast. If you're camera ready, get it on YouTube, TikTok, and/or IG Reels. If all you have the bandwidth for is once a week availability then make it the same day, same time every week. Then be sure to go back and engage with the audience. If you leave them hang'n, they will leave alone, PERIOD.

6. Confirmation Bias

Folx wanna know that they're right so they seek out someone who can confirm it. Everything you've done; framing, anchoring, representing, and being available, confirms for the audience that they're right, not you. You said it the right way, with the right anchor, with the right representation, at the right time. It's like a perfect storm to them. But you have to take the good with the bad. The same thing that makes folx love you, will make other folx hate you, and that's okay. The best thing to do is maintain the personal brand, don't make it personal.

The brain can process more than one bias so use intersectionality to your advantage. The more you know who you attract, the more you can tap into their intersectional biases. Let's look at a few.

Affect/Framing Bias

- Emotional Framing: Carefully selected words/tone to get at specific emotions.
- Emotional Anchoring: Strong emotional story to frame a specific.

Anchoring/Representation Bias

- Breaking Stereotypes Anchor: Challenging what folx in your industry should look or sound like.
- Visual Anchoring: Using imagery to project a look and vibe.

Affect/Framing/Anchoring/Representation Bias

- Younique Broadcast: How you make the audience feel (affect) with what you say (framing) so it's remembered (anchoring), using your hyphens, strengths, and language (representation) can position you ten toes down. It's up to the audience to decide if they like it or not..

Instead of fixing your face to people please, you position your personal brand to stand. Understand that bias intersectionality is your marketing gold mine when you amplify the broadcast with it.

1. How can you affect the ATM?

_____

_____

_____

2. How will you frame your broadcast?

_____

_____

_____

3. Where and how will you drop anchor content?

_____

_____

_____

4. What is your archetype mix and why?

_____

_____

_____

5. Where, when and how often are you available?

_____

_____

_____

6. How will you maintain confirmation bias?

_____

_____

_____

The art of broadcasting a biased message is a sophisticated mix of youniqueness, psychology, and strategy. When you understand yourself, you understand the ATM you attract. Maintaining an amplified message they can relate too will increase your attractiveness.

Everybody, and they momma, knows the ATM is where the money resides. Broadcasting the right message, at the right time, consistently is how you get them to pay attention to the point of coming outta pocket. Don't get distracted and discouraged by the three second rule.

It's your level of dedication that establishes the personal brand reputation. And as a service based business your audience will ebb and flow. And because you broadcast the same message with the same promise and conviction, it makes the reviews and testimonials make sense.

Broadcast a message that endorses the business so your audience doesn't see you as the business; the only one in your company who can get the job done. Your role as a brand leader is to lead and that herd may be hiding your first hire.

**Make people believe who you are
before they see you.**

- Snoop Dogg on Big Boy TV

Publicizing Over Projection

Back in the church days of my youth I sang in the church choir. During rehearsal my cousin, the choir directress, would always tell us to project from the diaphragm. And as we sang she would walk to the last pew to make sure we were projecting. If she thought we were holding back, she would make each person hit a note to see if she could hear us in the back row.

I have a choir voice; nice, loud alto. Me singing a solo part at church is like making sure every kid gets a swing at bat. But there is something about singing gospel that just feeds your spirit. So when cousin would ask me to hit a note, I would open my mouth and project. In that moment, all that mattered was giving glory to God.

Not being good as something doesn't mean you can't love it and I love singing. Once I did karaoke of Proud Mary at a clients catered event. Little did I know one of our servers was recording. Baby, I was channeling my inner Tina Turner and I did not care.

Then something unexpected happened to shake my spirit. I was part of the worship team at my last church singing as a loud alto like I had done for years. One day after rehearsing a particular song one of the lead singers said to me, "Remind me not to sing next to you anymore."

That statement brought took me back to when folx told me to

stop being so damn loud. And every time I saw her at rehearsal I was reminded that I was too loud and she was a better singer. After a while I began to skip rehearsals until I eventually left the worship team.

Although this is my second time mentioning my faith it is very personal to me. I don't publicize it because it's not part of the GCB or BH brand. What I publicize is a promise to stay true to self while lifting others. I publicize that I no longer believe in the you are your brand philosophy. I publicize that personal life and personal brand should have clear boundaries. I don't want anyone to feel like they can't sing.

Having a broadcast where you publicize a promise, you position as a show, not tell personal brand. It impacts everything from your message to your marketing. If you see what I see, you know there are Founders who are loud. It's like sitting in a car with the windows rolled up while you sing at the top of your lungs. Folx will walk by and see you do'n your thing. But they never stop long enough to see what you're singing.

I would rather see you as a Founder who is bold enough to post up outside the car. Publicize your song. Now folx are stopping, not all but enough. A few of the ones who stop give you money. And because you're amplifying the broadcast, those that can see you can still hear you.

That song is your promise. It keeps you true to you and those you serve. That's what you publicize. You no longer have to project and make irrelevant announcements.

Watching you put your business in the streets in an effort to be authentic is old and tired. Photos next to luxury items ain't fool'n nobody. Yaa, you lost fifteen pounds. No one who's looking for a solution really cares. It's all a projection of what you think folx wanna see and hear.

Have you ever heard the phrase, "Word is bond?" I always hear it in Morris Chestnut's voice when he was in The Best Man. It's so simple and yet so powerful. Being a person of your word is the most important part of your reputation. That's how you build trust and respect. It's tied to the level of Dedication found in your C.O.D.E. and comes through the core message.

When I committed to being part of the worship group, I made a promise to show up for rehearsals. When I lost the joy being in the group brought me I broke my promise. I was committed to being part of the group but I was dedicated to it. If I were dedicated, what the other person said wouldn't have broken my spirit.

Dedication is driven by internal motivation, not outside expectations. That's because it's based on something you truly believe in. It takes the guess work out of commitment. Putting dedication before commitment positions your personal brand to publicize a promise you can keep. And you don't have to fix your face to do it.

Committing to a promise without dedication makes you feel trapped. It's a mindset shift of have to instead of want to. You feel obligated and pressured by the promise and that leads to things like procrastination or stagnation. Whatever pie in the sky thoughts you had when you made the promise become a burden of obligation that burns you out and steals your joy.

After a while, that sense of obligation stresses you the fuck out.

You've just crossed over from burden to ball and chain. You're slowly dragged into being a people pleaser. That freedom you worked so hard for is gone. The joy you brought to the personal brand is sucked dry because the promise has more to do with commitment than dedication.

As if that weren't enough, the obligation to keep the promise has you procrastinating on what you publicize. Do you know how much time, energy, and resources are required to procrastinate? You're constantly playing catch up only to fall further behind. You've gone from Founder to employee who puts out the fires. You committed your brand to a promise you thought "THEY" wanted. And by they I mean the audience.

Your publicized broadcast causes you to build resentment. That resentment bleeds into your personal life and non-business relationships. If ever there was an example of your mouth writing a check your ass can't cash (or doesn't want to), a committed promise is it. You lose the genuine willingness to keep the promise because you feel imprisoned by it. Your personal brand infringes on your personal freedom.

Publicizing and amplified broadcast is easier when it's based on a dedicated promise. It's near and dear to your heart. Nothing outside of a life and death decision would make you pull up roots, unlike a stand alone commitment.

How many times have you heard someone commit to something publicly on to have take it back? How many times have you seen public figures make can apologies because they made a public ass of themselves? Now we have a world of folx afraid of being canceled. They publicize carefully crafted bullshit because they're living paycheck to paycheck.

Dedication to the promise means you're all in on the outcome. You're motivated by the intrinsic things of life and not just the money. It also taps into the purpose fulfillment. So now when you take action to keep the promise you get an empowering and rewarding feeling. You're not just going through the motions. You're making it make sense for you and not just your audience. You get to engage in a way that aligns with how you want to live. Now that's freedom.

Publicizing a message based on a dedicated promise doesn't feel like a commitment. Instead, it feels like you're on a path that contributes to your sense of autonomy and control. You're not pressured by folx on the outside or their expectations. You get to brand by example based on your own inner compass.

On top of that, the dedicated promise keeps you resilient so you can persevere against haters. When someone comes for you with obstacles and challenges, you take them on as step'n stones. You reassert your dedication and don't let them beat you or weigh you down. Your publicize broadcast is recycled motivation and satisfaction giving you less balls to juggle in life.

While you're publicizing a message with promise and genuine desire, you're also increasing your joy and your freedom. The connection of life, brand, and business are evident. So are the boundaries between your personal life and your personal brand. You're engaging in a way that allows you to experience a deeper sense of purpose, a deeper sense of self, and a deeper sense of gratitude for getting paid to do something you love.

No one can steal your joy because you're singing a song you wrote. You're not diminished because someone else has a better voice. And those who stop and pay attention don't give a rats ass if you hit all the right notes. You're able to engage with them because they're attracted to the broadcast.

In essence, when a brand promise is driven by dedication and a genuine desire, it becomes a source of increased joy and freedom. Joy and freedom are attractive qualities because they come across as confidence. This positive engagement with the audience transforms the nature of the responsibility. And you experience a increased sense of purpose, autonomy, fulfillment, and profits.

The promise you make as a Founder flows through the entire brand architecture. It affects the way you lead, hire, and expand. It is your ten toes down line in the sand. Everything you do within your business is about fulfilling the promise so it becomes a show instead of a tell. That's publicizing.

Publicizing the brand promise as part of a larger message is a reminder to you and the audience how you do what you do. And while everyone else is relying on trust by way of exposing their personal life, you're earning respect by upholding the promise. And respect breeds trust.

1. What resources, support, and/or actions do you have access to for fulfilling the promise?

_____

_____

_____

_____

2. What soft skill or character trait surfaces when you make a passionate statement about what you're dedicated to?

_____

_____

_____

_____

3. What type of promise would come across as genuine and ring true using the youniqueness factor of your personal brand?

_____

_____

_____

_____

4. So what's your promise?

_____

_____

_____

_____

Most folx can spot fake and fuckery a mile away. They may never speak on it, but that doesn't mean they don't see it. So to project your lifestyle and not expect judgement is ridiculous. I often say, personal branding is not personal. That's doesn't mean it won't have an emotional impact.

There are parts of your life that become part of the brand broadcast. Choosing whats relevant keeps you from making it overly personal. Wanting to share your joy, pain, and turmoil is not what your audience is for, unless it's related to the promise of the brand.

This is about staying true to you, not fixing your face for others. So just know:

- Publicizing a promise that you can stay dedicated to is broadcasting your truth
- When you broadcast from a dedicated place, you're tapping into your freedom, purpose, and joy.
- You avoid people-pleasing mentality when you're dedicated to the promise you want to commit to.

"The streets will teach you about racism and capitalism and survival of the fittest. Don't worry about that. The only thing you've got to worry about is if you've got enough cold-blooded ambition to apply the lessons you get taught."

- *Snoop Dogg*

BRIDGES

Bridges are built to make connections and to get over and around obstacles. That sounds like a great job for a personal brand. Being a brand instead of building one is you being an obstacle instead of a bridge.

Let's do a remix with the chicken crossing the road and the information super highway. Instead of asking, "Why did the chicken cross the road," ask, why did the chicken cross the information super highway? It's because there was no bridge.

Every time your folx try to cross the road, they're run over with information. Positioning yourself as a brand you're waving from across the road. And you've gone from chickens crossing roads to playing a game of Frogger.

Instead of trying to fix your face as an expert, position your personal brand as an endorser.

Getting To The Other Side

There was a time when saying, "There's nothing between us but space and opportunity" meant, I'm ready for a fight. That was the world I grew up in. You could double down on the statement with, "I'm right here, whatchu gone do?" You're either gonna put up or shut up.

Announcing that there's space and opportunity is one of the boldest position you can take outside of an actual threat. You stand your ground and spread your arms wide for effect. You're sure you'll win, otherwise why bother making the announcement? In business, it's an approach that leverages expertise with a show instead of tell.

You can't go back to "selling wolf tickets" unless you have a predilection for starting fights you can't win. You also don't want to look like a punk in front of everybody. If we share a similar background, you know the mental gymnastics required to not feel like you're being dared to fight. Especially when you had to fight for damn near every good thing in your life?

Let's revisit Snoop for a minute. Dude went from the streets of the LBC to rep'n America at the Olympics in Paris. Who saw that coming? Does it have anything to do with his connection to Martha? Is she the space and opportunity provider of his growth?

Truth be told, don't know, don't give a fat rats ass.

Fo shizzle Snoop had to put some skin in the game at various points of his career. Building bridges to take advantage of space an opportunity is not done on a whim, and not without work. The work didn't hinder his Crip walking or weed smoking. Talk about not fixing you face for a mutha f...

When it comes to actual bridges I am a new box of crazy. Yes, I suffer from acrophobia, a fear of heights. I get nauseous looking at my screen when that guy is climbs the radio tower. And I ride glass elevators facing forward as close to the door as possible. But as much as it bothers me whenever I cross a bridge I have to look down, if possible.

On a trip to the bay area I walked across the Golden Gate Bridge with my cousin. Anxiety of an earthquake plagued me with every step, and yet, I wanted to look down. And being tall I'm always worried about low rails, and yet, I still want to look down. What in the fresh hell is wrong with me?

Going from one end of the bridge to the other and back accomplished nothing. I scared the shit out of myself just so I could say I crossed the bridge on foot. Now put your audience in my shoes. How many potential clients have made it all the way up to your key offer and turned around to go back? Of course I'm speaking metaphorically, but we've all experienced it in one way or another. So what's up with bridges that fill **space and opportunity?**

When it comes to personal branding, there is plenty of both.

You occupy space with an amplified broadcast. Opportunities to leave a mark come from your reinforced boundaries. Using those combined assets to build a multi-lane bridge is what closes the gap between the audience and the offer. Let's name those lanes **Prop**, **Drop**, and **Pop** which I'll come back to.

Founders who are of the, I am my brand, variety broadcast a message of "social proof." Every time they get an award, a mention in a magazine, or sit on a panel, they're put'n it out there. This falls in the "market or hype yourself" advice column. They use space and opportunity to flex. The audience may applaud that, but it doesn't benefit from it so they turn around.

If all you want to do is hype or market yourself, Sweetheart, you don't need a personal brand for that. The self-employment vs. entrepreneurship argument applies here. Hyping yourself aligns with employed folx who believe they need a personal brand to climb the corporate ladder.

It's like the micromanager who derives self-importance from their position. They get all the credit for work done by others. They position themselves as obstacles instead of bridges. They create problems instead of solutions. They're afraid someone is trying to make them look bad.

Separating yourself from all the employee bullshit you left behind is like every other life onion you've had to peel. It doesn't just disappear when you turn in your two week notice. It takes time that most aren't willing to put in. And even as you build a new bridge, there are some old ones in your past you have to burn.

The who, what, and how of your broadcast gets a lotta folx to your bridge. That's how the personal brand takes the leadership position. If you lead them to a place where the space is filled with your hyped bullshit then you're creating obstacles in place of opportunity.

Going back to Snoop, the obstacles of his old lifestyle are not that far behind him. His glorified thug life is an obstacle for many. His best friend, Tupac was gunned down. He got hit with a murder charge and sat in prison for three years. But if not for that prison term we would've missed "Murder Was The Case They Gave Me." None of that has stopped hindered is brand. Did I already mention the love he got in Paris during the 2024 Olympics?

When Snoop decided to "rebrand" you could see the redirect. It even impacted his music and he wasn't top'n the charts like before. He went from Snoop Dogg to Snoop Lion for a while. It's what Big Boy said when he interviewed him in April 2023. Snoop "you're paying tuition into the school of experience." And he did it while the world with a blunt while the world watched. Whether you're a fan or not, you've witnessed folx going against the norm to embrace his personal brand. It created space and opportunity for others to enter the Dogg Pound life.

Going through hours of Snoop's interviews, there's something most miss or ignore. He doesn't flex what he has in the way of accolades and awards. He does, however, own the brilliance of what he does and what's it's meant for his career. He continues to mature as he goes from Snoop Dogg to Uncle Snoop. All the while his personal brand as Snoop Dogg does not inflict on his personal life as Calvin Broadus, Jr.

Snoop doesn't give a fuck about know, like and trust. His personal brand is built on respect. Even when he wrote the song, "I Wanna Thank Me," it wasn't done as self-promotion or hype. He was respecting his roll in the game. He was talking about the hard work, faith, and hours he put into his career.

How many autobiographies have you read about someone making it out of the hood, or the trailer park, or the slums. We all love a good under dog story. And Snoops is no different. He's an icon and a legend. His boundaries and broadcast have resulted in an expectation that whatever he touches turns to gold.

In the interview I mentioned earlier, Big Boy said, "We know Snoop. We know the brand. I can't even say rapper Snoop because there's so many different Snoops that I can say as far as hashtags and asterisks." He knows his expertise in the game of business. The bridge between them is so well constructed between the audience and the personal brand he never says Calvin.

It's the show and not the tell of personal brand positioning. It's a narrative that sucks you in with evidence of triumph. There are folx with financial means and privilege to buy their way into the rap game who achieve nothing. They could ask the same questions as you, "Why him and not me?" He built a bridge money can't buy.

Go back in the book to where you identified your strengths.

When you read through them, see the potential, not the lack. It doesn't matter how much life has beat you up. Every success in your life is a crawl before you walk moment.

You know bridges scare the fuck out of me, especially ones over water. But I can't help but look out, from the middle lane of course. But folx have to cross bridges. Or rather they should. To go a different way is to go the long way or not to go at all.

Expertise that's required to build and maintain a bridge between the audience and the offer no longer requires you to fix your face. Neither does it require you to kiss ass or people please. At this stage of the game you want folx to know what to expect when they do business with your company, not you. You're an expert on what your business does well because you started it. You've worked or you're working your way out of the day-to-day grind but maintaining the bridge is long-term.

If you've been around the employment block a few times, you've witnessed at least one micro manager. A person who takes up space not as an expert but an asshole afraid of feeling unimportant. They get salty when they think someone beneath them doesn't deserve a position above them. This happens when business owners feel trapped by the business they started because they're afraid to let someone else run it.

In the game of business today, intellectual property is your bread and butter. And loss of IP is a real fear for a lot of service-based business Founders. Your default marketing ends up being a tell instead of show branding model. You're afraid showing too much, someone will steal your IP and make the money you feel you're entitled to. It was rumored that happened more than once on Clubhouse when some well-known entrepreneurs showed up.

I know for a fact someone bought the domain <u>ghettocountry-brandmother.com</u> during my days on Clubhouse. That's because I visited rooms that were all about buying and selling domains for passive income. They thought they had me. I only looked it up the url out of curiosity.

It didn't matter to me that someone else bout the url. I already owned the registered trademark and it's too fucking long for a url. But the kicker was that whoever bought it couldn't do shit with it accept hold it. They banked on me wanting to buy it and they lost. Eventually they let it go and it's still available to this day.

It just goes to show that even if someone tries to take what's yours it doesn't diminish the value of your brand. It also doesn't devalue your expertise in the game. That's why your personal brand needs to take advantage of the space an opportunity that exists to build a multi-lane bridge between your offer and your audience.

Now let's take it back to the top where I mentioned the "Prop, Drop, and Pop." These are the three broadcasting lanes that make up your personal brand bridge. They integrate expertise and endorsement in a way that provides information and connection between the audience and the offer. They break down like this:

- **Prop:** This lane is a double dip of value prop and giving props, leveraging your education and expertise with your lived experience. It's an approach where you're not just listing your hyphens in bios. You're capitalizing on your youniqueness. As a personal branding expert, for example, being raised hood adjacent by a country mama has given me a younique flavor of challenges faced by rebellious founders who are not part of the mainstream narrative.
- **Drop:** In this lane you drop the mic as a niche of one. This is where you go big and you go home. You drop knowledge, value, and practical advice surround offer and your industry using your youniqueness. It's where you share a bit of yourself as part of a bigger picture. Not by being a brand but by building a whole brand architecture because of the youniqueness of one. In turn you attract clients and a culture who want to spend money and time with you.
- **Pop:** This final lane is where you make it pop with emotion. It doesn't require a library of emotional terms. You just need to leverage one emotion that's true to you. One that can be explained a thousand different ways. That emotional tether is an anchor and affect bias that helps the audience make a quick decision. That emotion is tied to the why of it all. It's the emotional high of why you do what you do and who you do it for. And that's why the audience wants to get high with you.

Building a bridge like this takes time and it's never-ending because new folx are always looking for you. You haven't reached celebrity status yet so there's an untapped audience still looking. And being **Dedicated** to who you are and what you bring to the game is a requirement is how you retain value. And on top of that, when someone tells you to stay in your lane, you can ask, "Which one?"

Broadcasting to the world that you are the brand is equivalent to standing on a bridge and blocking the way. It comes from the continuous bad advice of market yourself. There is a time and place to talk about your education, expertise, and lived experience. Using it to fill your content calendar is not it. It just obstructs the view of the offer. Only so many folx are willing to go around the obstruction to see what's on the other side.

You don't get respect if you don't
deserve it.

- *Snoop Dogg*

Drop The Mic

The bar for being profound has dropped so low you can't limbo under it without being double jointed. Even if you're re-gurgitating nonsense, someone who hasn't heard it all before will think you're "drop'n gems." Positioning your personal brand with a mic drop message means you tackle an issue with a niche of one perspective, go deep with it, and become a trusted authority around that issue.

Look at it this way. Your personal brand is a niche of one in the overall brand architecture of your business. The credibility you garner around a mic drop message makes you an undis-puted authority. You spoke your truth and that makes it genuine, not authentic. You now own the space.

During my Bigmista day's we started saying, "Drop it like it's hot," whenever someone asked for our spicy sauce. Eventually, that how folx began ordering. As our business grew and our lines got longer we switched it up.

To ease the stress of long lines and long waits, whoever was on the board that day would yell out, "Who wants a sample?" Of course hands would fly up. In response the carver would come back with, "Drop it like it's hot." Our regulars knew what that meant. It's not a mic drop, but watching folx have fun and getting special treatment for it was our thing.

But where did we get the phrase, "Drop it like it's hot?" Snoop, of course. And while we weren't expecting folx to do it video vixen style, many had fun trying. Now I want you to think about this. Not everyone had ever heard Snoop's version of drop it like it's hot. And yet that doesn't diminish his personal brand or the Snoop empire.

Snoop is not a one hit wonder. That's because his music is full of mic drop moments that resonate with folx. Rap is where he planted his flag and it's the hill he'll die on. It's has nothing to do with filling gaps and asking why. It goes back to *Dedication* and staying true to you. It's an offensive defense. If you can be swayed, pushed, or bullied to change your position, then that is not your hill.

Coming up with the right remix to reinforce your boundaries provides a *younique* perspective to your education and expertise, allows you to *connect* on a deeper level, and you build trust as an authority in the game. What is that powerful and impactful topic that you can dominate. And don't get it twisted. This is about change, not opinion.

Let's go back to your perspective. It is your background and lived experience that shape your approach to the industry. It's this younique perspective that positions your personal brand as a game changer when all other alternatives are basic and generic.

Instead of yammering about the same shit as everyone else or jumping on trends, be bold enough to state your change.

We already know folx are willing to steal basic bullshit. They can't steal your youniqueness. You question norms, challenge bullshit and you innovate. All this is true to you.

Again, you are not trying to fill a gap, but you're also not trying to be different for the sake of being different. You're lending value to an industry that needs to change in some shape, form, or fashion. You're providing insights and ingenuity to something that's not right for whatever reason.

And because of younique message is based on your lived experience, you can back it up. You're not talking in theory or hyperbole, you're spit'n facts and you know them. This strengthens your credibility and makes your mic drop moments that much more persuasive.

And here's where you get emotional, not personal. Because this is a whole ass situation for you, you're aligned and connected to what you offer. That emotion is picked up by the audience. They connect with it because you're not giving okie doke energy, which they can get anywhere. That emotion taps into their heuristic bias so they keep coming back.

It doesn't matter that you're not caught up in the day-to-day. It matters that you're leading the day-to-day so everyone comes to the same conclusion; they need/want to do business with you. Yes, folx are attracted to fame and fortune. That is until you wind up in the "What ever happened to..." discard pile. But when your genuineness shows, like Snoop dancing at the Olympics, folx see past the glitz and glamour.

Now we get to you being a trusted authority in the game. Having mic drop moments happen when you least expect them. You're not putting on a show for the folx. You're provided value and insights for the audience based on your Youniqueness. As a niche of one Brand Leader, you put in the work to earn, not expect, trust.

Folx keep telling you that attentions spans have shortened. You hear the same noise about your industry being crowded and saturated. The reasons you may believe this is:

1. Everyone says you have 3-seconds to get the audience's attention. Did you ever stop to consider that folx have gotten bored with the same-o same-o. Watching or listening to you do what's already been done adds no value to their existence.
2. Being new to the game, you surrounded yourself with folx who do the same thing you do. You wanted to learn and understand your industry. Once you know enough to step out of the industry shadow, you don't know how because you're surrounded by so-called competition.
3. You feel like you don't measure up and the algorithm is working against you. Most of what you see are "hyping" themselves and telling you to be "authentic." You don't really know what that means so you stamp imposter syndrome across your forehead and where it like a badge of honor.

It's hard to find your "mic drop" moments when you believe all that bullshit is working against you. As Lisa Nichols would say, "That ain't none a yo business," literally and figuratively speaking. When you switch the focus from *differentiation* to niche of one (worrying about your own self), the rest of it doesn't matter. You silence the crowd because they have to pick the lower lip up off the floor.

Folx will cross a bridge, an ocean, and a universe when they feel it's for the right reason or in your case, the right personal brand. Your ten toes down amplified broadcast is that reason because when you drop the mic, it's genuine, not trendy or regurgitated quotes from famous folx. You're not afraid to challenge the status quo.

If you're gonna do a mic drop, you may as well drop it like it's hot. By crafting a mic drop narrative you make it known you're not afraid to stand on a hill alone. Your reinforced boundaries and broadcast have created space and opportunities for you to do just that.

As a brand leader, you are not the narrative, you control it. Turning yourself and your life into the mic drop of it all is to position as a commodity to be bought and sold. This hinders the profitability and sustainability of a growing brand and business that keeps you shackled to the day-to-day grind of it all.

Mic drops are not manufactured to keep up with trends and popularity. Sometimes only the audience will see it as a mic drop. As the Brand Leader and endorser of all sub-brands you bring value and credibility which get's passed along to the business.

Folx who wanna cross a bridge look to you for actionable insights and strategies. This is not your secret sauce for making money. This is persuasive copy that translates to something actionable they can do themselves. You broadcast practical advice for the masses and save the specific advice for the clients.

My husband is constantly telling me to, "take the horn out cha mouth." That's because I have a tendency to talk to much. But the trip part is folx will say things like, "I can listen to you all day." So should I shut up or speak up? I guess it would depend on who you ask.

I amplify a core message of people not being brands because they're to brilliant. I back that up by reflecting their lives back at them, the things they've accomplished, the challenges they've met, the hurdles they jumped. Again, that's being not a brand, it's the brilliance and resilience of you. I could talk about that shit all day, everyday. I can develop a strategic personal brand around it.

Not being a brand is my constant mic drop message for the masses. It's backed by practical advice on why that's a thing. My clients get a more specific message and nurturing on why it's not a thing for them. Because that's my focus folx will often comment I'm drop'n gems. Those gems are just more mics falling.

When you go deep instead of wide with a message, you get off the basic bus. You're showing that you know what you're talking about and why it matters. Being that trusted no-nonsense resource positions your personal brand as a leader, an expert, and an authority. Bring some innovation to the game and you're now considered a thought leader.

All of this creates space and opportunity for a repository of knowledge. That's because the deeper you go, the more refined your message. Those who follow in your footsteps will be cheap imitations by comparison because you were first on the scene. No more creating courses and bullshit books that lead to more bullshit. Your repository is filled with original work and all those you learned from become footnotes in what you now offer.

By continuously dropping knowledge bombs and reinforcing a brand architecture on your youniqueness, you continue to attract folx who want to work with you and for you. It's a dynamic culture creation that transforms your courage into confidence.

You can't be afraid to drop the mic and walk away. You can't be afraid of standing alone for a while. The personal brand will do the heavy lifting if you have the courage to do the rest.

1. What younique perspective do you bring to the industry or market that is not self-serving?

_____

_____

_____

_____

_____

2. What is your opinion on the change or impact that needs to happen that your offer addresses within the industry or market?

_____

_____

_____

_____

_____

3. How can you offensively defend your position as an authority of a younique perspective that goes against the status quo?

_____

_____

_____

_____

_____

Mic drops start with you stepping up to lead the charge of change. Leveraging your youniqueness earns you the trust of the ATM so they cross the bridge. They in turn attract others. Don't become an obstacle on the bridge by tapping into your personal life when it holds no relevance for them.

You don't have to fix your face to become a trailblazer. Leave that to the trend followers. Know when you drop the mic and capitalize on it. Go deep with it, not wide. Find that lone hill and stand ten toes down. Just because you're there alone doesn't mean no one's watching.

This is where you earn the recognition. The more value you and, the greater the brand equity of your business. As the leader you continue to control the narrative. It's like a never-ending story of growth for the company. And because you dropped the mic first, your own story is deeply rooted in the sustainability of it all.

"You've got to always go back in time
if you want to move forward."

- Snoop Dogg

Prop The Message

All you gentle parents may wanna skip this story because as a product of my upbringing, I believe in butt whoop'ns as a form of punishment. It's one of the reasons I don't make light of my parental promises.

I am a mother of many chances but once I promise my daughter consequences, I have to follow through, the same way I would follow through on a promise of something good. My daughter has known this ever since she was a toddler. Did it always work out in her favor? No.

I remember very vividly an impromptu trip we made to San Diego. It was me, Morgan, who was eight at the time, my mom and stepdad on a sunny Sunday afternoon hitting the 405. No plans to really see or do anything, just something to get my mom out the house.

While we were there we did some touristy type shopping. In this one store my daughter asked me could she have this little toy. I told her no because I knew she would lose it. She begged and promised she wouldn't. I kept saying no until my mom intervened. She told me to stop being a mean to her baby and get it for her.

I stared my mom in the eye for about five seconds before

turning to Morgan and asking, "Morgan, do you really want it that bad?" She said yes with a big grin and my heart was already breaking because I know how careless my daughter could be.

As a last ditch deterrent I said, "Okay, but Morgan, if you lose this before we get home I promise you I'm gonna whoop your butt." I had never broken a promise to my daughter.

Without thinking she said okay and grabbed the little toy. She had no pockets or purse to put it in so I asked if you wanted me to hold it. She said no and closed her hand real tight. Thinking about it even now hurts my heart. I don't blame her or my mom, but the deal was set.

Where some moms would say, "Don't make me tell you again," my mom used to say, "I can show you better than I can tell you. Keep it up." It's a threat equivalent to fuck around and find out. The value proposition of that promise was loud and clear, unlike, "Don't make me tell you again."

If your momma was like my momma, once she got up to act on her promise, there were not enough apologies in the world to make her not follow through. Right now she's in my head saying, "That's because folx don't believe fat meat is greazy." And yet their grandkids are the exception.

That's the thing about making promises, everyone expects you to keep them until they need an exception. When you back up your amplified broadcast with a promise, your audience expects you to follow through. You've consistently told them your policies, procedures and prices. But there's always someone who will have the audacity to ask for an exception on everything from price to product.

No one **EVER** expects you to really be an "asshole" when they're asking you for a favor. I'm here to tell you that you have to be that asshole. And when you are, you're talked about like a dog because you kept your promise. They make their problem your problem.

You know you're not really an asshole but you feel shitty nonetheless. Your humanity is telling you to discount your price, give them some extra, do it just this once. But once turns into more than once very quickly because they went and told their friends how they got over on you.

I don't know if it's relevant today or in other cultures, but when it comes to a black woman's hair stylist, she never tells how much she's charged. That's because the same person has been doing her hair for years, and she's earned the financial favors she provided. To make others privy to that favor is grounds for finding a new stylist. I had my last stylist for almost twenty years before I went short.

There's nothing wrong with making exceptions for clients, you just don't make it part of the broadcast. What is part of the broadcast is the promise you prop it up with. It's cemented to the brand. To waiver would be to weaken the trust of the bridge. Folx may forgive you for a broken trust but they seldom forget.

Words not backed by a promise are hollow and meaningless. A promise not backed by action is a straight up lie. Folx are tired of tell and want to see you show up for what you're trying to sell them. So if you're gonna make a bridge mic drop, you gotta prop it up with a promise you can keep.

When it comes to personal brand positioning, the promise is in the value prop. A promise that supports the intended outcome makes sense and will mean all the things to the audience. Also, that promise doesn't need to be the same as the one for the business, but it must be aligned. It's what makes the mic drop so poignant.

Propping up the bridge of a broadcast does not require you to run around posting content using the words, "I promise…" Remember, personal branding is a show, not tell game. And showing you can keep a promise has more value than announcing the promise.

Folx who hype themselves announce a promise and expect it to prop up their content, not the value of the brand. Their LinkedIn profiles read like either a hyphen grocery list or a bad case of the "helps." I help {insert bullshit} do {insert bullshit} by {insert more bullshit}. It's a mission statement gone wrong.

In short, a value proposition is like a friends with benes arrangement. Okay, maybe that's a bit much. But still, most are made up from a sample template used by every new entrepreneur ever. They don't know why they need to make the statement, they just fill in the template blanks.

Plain and simple, it's you making a promise to do something that benefits someone else. When you base that promise on filling a gap or trying to be different it sounds as bland as unseasoned chicken.

Promises can have a negative benefit like the one I made to my daughter. On our way back to San Diego we made plans to meet my husband at a downtown Long Beach restaurant. After we ordered I asked my daughter about her toy. Her face was an instant mask of regret. Because I didn't want to keep my promise, I even helped her look for it.

I asked her, "Have I ever broken a promise," and she said no. I said, "So I have to keep this promise even though it's not a good one. All through dinner and in the car my mom was trying to convince me to not go through with it. Even though she was the reason Morgan got the toy, she was just being a Grandma.

When we pulled into our driveway, Morgan was sleep and my heart was heavy. I woke her up and as soon as she saw the house she went into instant sobs that were so hard and heart wrenching. She was yelling at herself for being stupid. And yet, I had to keep my promise. I was the asshole.

Talking with her afterwards I explained my actions and her expectations. Every time I promised her something good I came through. If I was ever unsure I would tell her, "We'll see." She's seventeen now. And although she's outgrown butt whoop'ns, we haven't grown out of keeping promises. But now they're pinky promises.

All those years earned me the trust of keeping a promise. I'm now privy to teenage fuckery that makes me want to stick my fingers in my ears. She has her share of secrets, but the ones she trust me with I don't even tell her dad without consent. The only caveat is if someone is in harms way, all bets are off.

Reinforcing relationships with promise after creating heuristic bias is positioning gold. The space you occupy in a persons mind makes you the talk of the town. In other words, they're giving you your "Props". It's how they show respect, admiration, or appreciation for you keeping or acting on your promise.

Consistently keeping your word exponentially amplifies a broadcast because you're no longer a lone voice. You maintain your niche of one status while folx in the audience prop up the bridge.

Earned props, like earned media, increase the level of trust which increases the personal brand equity. Respecting that it's not given lightly means you won't take it for granted. A promise kept, even in the face of consequence, solidifies your personal brand's position, not just in the mind, but in the life of prospects turn client.

Just as my relationship with my daughter has strengthened over time, despite occasional repercussions, so will your relationship with your audience. The core message of the brand is supported with a promise you can keep. In return you receive props from the available target market. That's a true value prop that surpasses marketing bullshit. It breeds loyalty by exceeding expectations. Earned props by others increases the impact of the broadcast and the influence of the personal brand.

This is not the old adage of under promise, over deliver. And it's not about some grandiose promise to show off. If you make it to heavy, you can't keep it. Simply make a promise you can fucking keep on the regular. Every so often show the audience how you kept it using a story, a testimonial, or a new offer. Promises are sacred, and don't let anybody tell you different.

1. What promise can you make that would benefit others?

_____

_____

_____

_____

_____

2. Why does keeping this promise matter to you and your business?

_____

_____

_____

_____

3. How will keeping this promise impacted those who will benefit?

_____

_____

_____

_____

Using a promise to back up the core message feeds into the biases formed by the brand. You see the benefit of it when you earn props in return. It's the ultimate social currency. You no longer have to rely on using words like premium or award winning. The ATM is giving you permission to price based on equity. It's uninhibited PR without the staging.

The freedom to give and receive props without fixing for face requires courage, patience, and time. It's a skill you cultivate as a self-aware Brand Leader who is genuine in the message delivery. And understanding the premise behind a promise that closes the gap between the audience and the offer, your growth, scalability, and expansiveness is free of encumbered bullshit.

A promise is a prop so you don't have to hype yourself. It widens the bridge and impacts income. If you resort to making it personal then the brand starts to crumble creating a domino effect of destruction.

"Sometimes, if you're lucky, someone comes into your life who'll take up a place in your heart that no one else can fill, someone who's tighter than a twin, more with you than your own shadow, who gets deeper under your skin than your own blood and bones."

- Snoop Dogg

Pop With Emotion

So here we are, at the metaphorical heart of the matter. The emotional side of branding. Without an emotional connection, none of this makes sense. But here's the irony of business. You're told to take emotions out of it. Don't take it personally. When it comes to personal branding, I only agree with one of those statements even though they seem inextricably connected.

There are moments when I feel like an empath on amphetamines. Getting caught up in the feelings of strangers is not an oddity for me. But because I know this, I've learned not to make it personal. The key word is LEARNED. That's why Ghetto Country Brandmother® is described as an empathic bitch.

Authenticity is THE buzzword for personal branding. It should be called a crutch word because folx use it as justification for making shit emotional and personal. You gotta know the difference between genuine emotion and taking shit personally. Once you can make the distinction, you can give your bridge a pop of emotion.

When you make it personal, you're saying it's all about you. You're the reason, the cause, the obstacle of everything that's going on, good, bad, or ugly. If you don't make the sell, you did something wrong. If you do make the sell you did something right. You are the reason for the success or failure of your business. Getting emotional about any of this is fine. Getting personal is not.

Marketing on any level is a waste of time if it has no emotional value. It's why so many folx think marketing is manipulative. I used to be one of those people. That was, until I understood more about how the brain makes quick decisions rooted in basic instincts guided by emotion.

There is so much to unpack because there's also the misguided notion of vulnerability on top of authenticity. The act of being vulnerable opens up a shit ton of personal interpretations. And because that act is so personal, any negative interpretation is taken personally. You watched Brené Brown's Ted Talk on vulnerability but did you ever take the time to read her book, Daring Greatly?

Using vulnerability to wear your heart on your sleeve is not emotional positioning. Leave that crazy for the I am my brand brigade. It is this type of emotionally personal advice that's contagiously conflicting and makes the authenticity argument moot. You have to reign in the personal and position strategically with the emotional so you can change the game of your inbound marketing.

It's no shocker that emotions create powerful connections. They can foster trust, loyalty, and favor. They can also foster anger, resentment, and prejudice. For example, a personal brand focused on social justice advocacy might share stories of personal struggle to make an emotional connection. The story will attract folx who champion social justice as well as those who don't believe injustices are occurring. And the way either of those camps engage with the stories can make you emotional. If you take the engagement personally then you're doing too much.

Sharing personal stories for content purposes requires a level of detachment. You're using your lived experience to connect with an audience, not to make a friend. Without detaching the personal you'll want to defend, justify, and argue when someone responds in a disagreeable manner. I know you want to fight me on this, in the name of authenticity, but why? Because you think you should? Because everyone else says so?

Making things personal can be detrimental to the position of the personal brand. You become more invested in the opinion or criticism about your person, and lose objectivity about the brand. Sharing stories that trigger that type of response are still to personal. And instead of being offensively defensive, you become defensively offensive. You want to justify and explain. That leads to emotional and personal responses that have no basis in business. This is why being a brand is problematic.

When emotional problems occur you hear folx complaining about always being on. Those are people who are trying to tap into manufactured or an abundance of emotions. They'll plaster on a fake persona and dole out what they deem appropriate for that content or marketing.

Being a neighborhood restaurant owner back in the day,

our customers would see me in my day-to-day life. They would instinctively greet me as Mrs. Mista and I would turn her on. It wasn't their fault. I allowed it and came to hate it.

Getting lost in being the brand is easy until you don't put an end to it. Slowly resentment becomes a dominant emotion and you start faking it. If you want to maintain your happy place, rely on an emotion you don't have to reach for. Reinforced boundaries, language, and promises help reveal the emotions you're comfortable with in your happy place. It's the one you keep in your back pocket even on your worst day.

My husband proudly proclaims he has four emotions; happy, horny, angry, hungry. Hungry is not an emotion, but I'm just trying to stay married today. So just know, if you make something feel like an emotion, roll with it. Anyway, in working with him to reintroduce the Bigmista brand, we tap into two of his four emotions; happy and hungry. This is true to him all day, er'ry day.

Bigmista's emotional side around food, booze, and travel focuses on taking the audience from hungry to happy or happy to hungry. Retaining this emotional space keeps him from over-sharing. Not that he ever would. This is his emotional comfort level. It also refines his broadcast message for greater resonance.

While Bigmista's emotional bent has a positive connotation, it doesn't mean you can't tap into the negative. But don't dish out what you can't handle. Narrowing down what emotions you bring to the message requires refinement. This is crucial because as a Brand Leader and Endorser you have to develop a thick skin. Tailoring your message around emotions you can handle better position the personal brand to deal with haters and not take it as a personal attack.

Despite limiting the emotions you bring to the personal brand message, the ones you do bring are genuine and trustworthy. This increases the space and opportunity to bridge the gap between the audience and the offer. It's not trickery or fuckery, and you definitely don't have to fix your face.

Manipulating feelings is not what's on the menu for you or the audience. Identifying the emotional triggers that drives you to do what you do deepen the connection. It doesn't matter if you label it passion or purpose. What matters is the emotion behind it that captures and motivates you to go from selfish to selfless. If you're frustrated, speak to your audiences frustration. If you're excited, speak to your audiences excitement. Doing to much would be like running through the house with emotional scissors.

Your core emotion becomes your personal brand's emotional tether, another hook to capture the audience. It deepens **affect bias**, which is the subconscious attraction you want folx to have with the personal brand. When your message hits on the emotional side with the own desires, frustrations, or aspirations, you've formed an emotional bond that tells them "this is the one!"

One core emotion can be the game changer behind the amplified message. It's the emotional high that structures content, shapes engagement, and becomes the why not to their why. It's your responsibility to handle with care, but you still can't make it personal. And even though this is not about you it doesn't stop someone from attacking you personally.

So let's go a bit further down the rabbit hole and look at through the lens of emotional intelligence, or EQ. Having the wherewithal to put your emotions in check is one part of it. The other part is recognizing and responding to the emotions of your audience. Choosing to engage on an emotional level you're not prepared for will throw you off your game. Instinctively you'll want to defend yourself.

If your goal is to bring a new emotion to the industry, this is not easy either. Don't expect folx to grasp the concept of something like anger and ice cream right away. You have to make it make sense for them. And it has to consistently be part of the amplified message. Just because you want to change how the game is played doesn't mean anyone is gonna play with you.

Let's go back to my husband for a sec. Horny can definitely fit into the food, booze, and travel of it all. Whip cream, chocolate covered strawberries, and honey are usual suspects in sexy scenes in movies and television. As I'm typing this I'm realizing horny is not an emotion. But I've been conditioned to view it as such because I've heard it for the past twenty years. But if it were an emotion, it's not one that could be sustained over long periods.

That's brings me to another point about EQ. It requires you to be self-aware, self regulatory, and socially skilled. Sustaining an emotion through out the personal brand experience is a must for the sake of consistency. Jumping from emotion to emotion is mentally draining which leads to burn out. And you can't expect others to accommodate your emotional triggers. Part of self- regulating is not going where you're not openly welcomed.

From a personal brand perspective you don't have to be part of every conversation. If you're personally triggered by a post, an article, or any type of content, respond as the person you are, not the personal brand. This is hard to do when your personal name is part of the equation. It's why I advocate for naming your personal brand, even if it's as basic as Coach Casey or Chef Charlotte. Dropping the coach or chef means you're living your life, not endorsing your business.

Positioning the personal brand with a pop of emotion keeps you from being emotionally drained. It doesn't require trauma dumping or spilling the tea on all your business. All you're looking for is a connection point that you can maintain with the ATM. Everything else you get to keep for yourself.

You're using your personal brand to build an empire, and you're tapping into some emotional shit. You have to handle with care because even though you can check yourself on not making it personal, you can't do it for others. You want to move people to take action so maintain a level of detachment and objectivity. After all, your personal brand is a business asset, and like any business you have to be emotionally intelligent and that transcends personal feelings.

1. What's the core emotion (or emotional mix) that happens in your happy place?

_____

_____

_____

_____

_____

2. How can this emotion (emotional mix) help your audience get to their desired emotion?

_____

_____

_____

_____

_____

3. How do I keep my emotions intact when personally attacked?

_____

_____

_____

_____

_____

Being an emotional creature doesn't mean you have to take everything to heart. And you don't want to be so engaged with your audience that money becomes an awkward conversation. Be strategic because this is business, not personal.

Separating your who from your do will take time and patience. Recognize that you're dealing with intellectual property. These are business assets that can be bought and sold, even if it's only an idea. And giving birth to an idea does not make it your baby.

Leveraging emotions for the sake of building a brand and running a business can be separate from how you live your life. Set emotional boundaries so you can show up consistently genuine. And don't engage with fuckery if it's going to trigger you and throw you off your game.

"Nobody ever got their ass out of the ghetto by letting someone else step ahead of them in line. And no-one ever got rich and famous by laying back and hoping someone would notice who they are and what they do."

- Snoop Dogg

WRAP IT UP

Metaphors aside, your business is how you make money, it's not who you are. Grasping at lofty titles to make yourself feel important is a vanity thing. It's pricing and reputation that hold determine positioning power, not the actual money you make or the title you hold

Brand positioning is not new to marketing but personal branding is new to positioning and brand architecture. And because folx didn't know how to handle it the personal brand integration, all they could say offer is, "market yourself." This served to turn you into a commodity and your life into content which diminishes your greatness as a human. It also puts you in the way of growing and expanding an empire. Your personal brand is influenced by your lived experience, however, displaying how you live your life is not a requirement.

Personal branding started as a means for climbing the corporate ladder. Folx thought it was a good idea to commoditize themselves in order to compete for the corner office. So you slap on a fake smile, "professional" demeanor, and call yourself a brand. In that context, positioning is about being seen by the "right" people with the right title.

After some time personal branding moved out of the corporate suites and into the mainstream of influencers, freelancers, and hustlers, better known as the self-employed. Everyone wants to be a brand, but no one ever thought to take it out of the corporate packaging. The act of being a self-employed commodity, it makes sense to hype and market yourself. And let's not forget, the whole thing about charging your worth. This type of talk is why I refer to branding as a pimp game.

Prostitution is prostitution, sweetheart. You're not selling sex, but you're still selling yourself instead of the result, solution or offer. Relying on yourself to make all the money is stressful as hell. Instead of taking a strategic approach to personal branding you turn your life into a side show of content because you're "A Brand." Why, so you can fix your face to chase money?

At the most basic level branding is about being remembered, being top of mind. Making the personal brand part of the overall brand architecture can make that happen and changes the dynamic of the personal brand. This change makes room to position the personal brand as an authority, expert, and leader. You can also position it for an exit. Positioning a business brand is different but there should be alignment between the two.

Personal brand positioning for entrepreneurs is not about fixing your face, it's about adjusting your attitude. You're in business because you want to give folx what they want, at a price point that's profitable. You don't have to kiss executive ass to get ahead. And the days of the customer is always right are over because as a Founder of a service-based business, the selection process is no longer one way.

Not fixing your face means you can be selfishly selfless. Position your personal brand to lead as an inbound marketing asset for the business. Use it to make unrelated markets relatable. Give it a name and license it for residual income instead of one and done brand deals. Endorse your business instead of hyping yourself.

Reinforcing boundaries, amplifying the core message, and bridging the gap between the audience and the offer is where you stand ten toes down as a leader. It's how you stay true to you as a level of self care. You can outgrow a personal brand if you choose. Or you can continuously use its credibility to endorse the sub-brands of the business.

Are you ready to consider your niche of one approach? Are you ready to give up algorithm chasing and content hustling? The future of personal branding is not in the hype and hustle of being a brand. It's in the space and opportunity of boundaries, broadcast, and bridges. Use yours for good so your business can grow, scale, and expand with genuine connection.

Building a branded house where every sub-brand is backed by the credibility of the personal brand is the new normal. Corporate games of competition are not necessary when you're not trying to taking over the world. Own the space as a niche of one and no will ever be able to compete with that. If they try, you know how small they really are.

ARCHETYPE
APPENDIX

LEAVE A LEGACY

OUTLAW
REVOLUTION

MAGICIAN
POWER

HERO
MASTERY

PURSUE CONNECTION

LOVER
INTIMACY

JESTER
LAUGHTER

EVERYMAN
BELONGING

PROVIDE
STRUCTURE

CAREGIVER
SERVICE

RULER
CONTROL

CREATOR
INNOVATION

EXPLORE SPIRITUALITY

INNOCENT
PURITY

SAGE
UNDERSTANDING

EXPLORER
FREEDOM

About Phyllis

Phyllis Williams-Strawder is a tough love force of nature in the world of strategic personal branding, coaching, and consulting. With a wealth of knowledge and a younique perspective, she challenges conventional wisdom, inspires real talk, and nurtures brandbaby founders to take control of their life, brand, and business.

Phyllis has certifications as a life, brand, business coach, a brand strategist, and one in marketing psychology. As a Brandmother, she brings a rare mix of education, expertise, and experience to the table.

Phyllis' journey to becoming the Ghetto Country Brandmother® is marked by her refusal to conform to industry norms. She doesn't take the word disrupter lightly. She's a truth-seeker and tireless advocate for putting folx first in the world of branding.

Phyllis hosts the "Branding, Boundaries, & Bullshit," podcast where she doesn't flinch from topics related to separating personal life from personal brand. Her unwavering ten toes down style make her a feared, yet fearless speaker.

theShadowLegacy

Interior and exterior of book design by
The Shadow Legacy

Also designers of:
Branding, Boundaries & Bullshit

www.theshadowlegacy.com
hello@theshadowlegacy.com

Other Books By The Author

Branding, Boundaries
& Bullshit

Brandma's Marketing Planner
For Shiny Object Chasers

Balance is Bullshit

Far From The Tree

That Damn Girl Stuff

Morgan Mischief

www.ingramcontent.com/pod-product-compliance
Lightning Source LLC
Chambersburg PA
CBHW020544270326
41927CB00006B/718